# COOL
## careers
### for
# girls

## in
# ENGINEERING

IMPACT PUBLICATIONS I

# COOL
## careers
### for
# girls
## in
# ENGINEERING

**CEEL PASTERNAK & LINDA THORNBURG**

**Liability/Warranty:** The authors and publisher have made every attempt to provide the reader with accurate information. However, given constant changes in the employment field, they make no claims that this information will remain accurate at the time of reading. Furthermore, this information is presented for information purposes only. The authors and publisher make no claims that using this information will guarantee the reader a job. The authors and publisher shall not be liable for any loss or damages incurred in the process of following the advice presented in this book.

**Library of Congress Cataloging-in-Publication Data**

Pasternak, Ceel, 1932-
    Cool careers for girls in engineering / Ceel Pasternak & Linda Thornburg.
        p. cm.
    Includes bibliographical references (p. ).
    ISBN 1-57023-126-5 (hbk.)—ISBN 1-57023-119-2 (pbk.)
    1. Women in engineering--Vocational guidance Juvenile literature. 2.
Women engineers--Vocational guidance Juvenile literature. 3. Women
engineers Biography Juvenile literature. I. Thornburg, Linda, 1949- II. Title.
Ta157.P325 1999

99-16717

CIP

**Publisher:** For information on Impact Publications, including current and forthcoming publications, authors, press kits, bookstore, and submission requirements, visit Impact's Web site: www.impactpublications.com

**Publicity/Rights:** For information on publicity, author interviews, and subsidiary rights, contact the Public Relations and Marketing Department: Tel. 703/361-7300 or Fax 703/335-9486.

**Sales/Distribution**: All paperback bookstore sales are handled through Impact's trade distributor: National Book Network, 15200 NBN Way, Blue Ridge Summit, PA 17214, Tel. 1-800-462-6420. All other sales and distribution inquiries should be directed to the publisher: Sales Department, IMPACT PUBLICATIONS, 9104-N Manassas Dr., Manassas Park, VA 20111-5211, Tel. 703/361-7300, Fax 703/335-9486, or E-mail: coolcareers@impactpublications.com

Book design by Guenet Abraham

*Dedicated to the women engineers,*
*who made our world a*
*better place to live.*

# Contents

**Professor of Aeronautics, Massachusetts Institute of Technology, Cambridge; Vice President, National Academy of Engineering, Washington, DC; and Former Secretary of the Air Force**

Look at the world around you. Why don't buildings fall down? Why do airplanes fly? Who makes sure that the things we use in our daily lives do what we want them to do and are safe to use? Engineers! Could you become an engineer? What do engineers do? And what does it take? How do you find out and how do you prepare? This book should answer some of these questions.

It was once very unusual for women to study and practice engineering. When I entered the Massachusetts Institute of Technology in Cambridge, we had 20 women in a freshman class of 1,000. Now the freshman class at MIT has 470 women in a class of 1,000. We have more women than men as undergraduate students in half of our engineering departments. Women are very much a part of the picture in engineering today. Big change!

How did I make the decision to become an engineer? Well, I love airplanes! I even like airplane noise. For me, the sight of an airplane flying above me is a constant source of wonder, excitement, and fascination. I never get tired of looking. I had the good fortune not only to be involved with airplanes as an aeronautical engineer, through my research and teaching, but also as Secretary of the Air Force, where I got to fly in essentially every airplane that is in the Air Force. I flew in fighters, bombers, transports, and helicopters. I flew with the Thunderbird demonstration team and pulled 9

g's. As Secretary of the Air Force, I also bought airplanes: quite a shopping trip! In my career, I've been associated with thousands of young people in aviation, who are passionate about what they're doing. But enough about me; what about you?

Your passion may not be airplanes or even space flight. You may have a passion to protect the environment, to make better products for people, to contribute to a healthy economy, to get involved with computers. The list goes on and on. You may also want to choose a career which will provide continuous challenges and good opportunities to make a difference.

The engineering careers in this book focus on a few of the potential kinds of careers for engineers. Engineers create new technologies, update existing technologies, and preserve old ways of doing things. Many people don't think about the fact that their lives depend a lot on engineering, and on engineers. But think about it. Engineers created the computer system that lets you play computer games at home and do school work on the Internet. Engineers also created your bicycle, the road you ride your bike on, and the safety helmet and stop light system that helps you ride safely. Every part of your life has been improved or changed by engineering.

Engineers work in many different places and do challenging and interesting work. Whether they work on designing the next generation car, speeding up your computer, cleaning the environment in your local park or river, creating new ways to help farmers grow crops with fewer pesticides, or designing machines to help people recover from serious injuries, engineers work to make people's lives better. Some engineers teach other engineers, some design machines and technologies, some do research, and many work out in the world of people every day. Engineering is a great field to be in because, wherever you live, jobs are usually available.

Engineering offers many options for careers, many rewards, and is just plain fun. If you like working with people, or exploring ways to do things faster and better, then engineering may be the career for you. In the United States, more than 1.3 million people work in engineering. (If you choose to explore a career in engineering, you will find plenty of options because there are many different engineering disciplines with many varieties of occupations today and new jobs are being created as technology changes.) Engineers usually work within a discipline, a specific area of engineering that they study in school. There are many disciplines to choose from— aerospace, automotive, biological, chemical, civil (buildings, bridges, roads, etc.), computer, electronic and electrical, power and energy systems, manufacturing, mechanical, and petroleum and mining.

## Getting Started Now

This book is a great place to start researching engineering careers. The stories of the women engineers in this book will give you a good idea of the educational requirements, a typical day, and the challenges and rewards of the many

different kinds of careers that they have chosen. You will also learn that some women made their career choices when they were girls. Along with each story, you will find a checklist with some clues about what type of personality would be suitable for a particular job. Information about salaries and employment opportunities is also provided.

The last chapter, Getting Started on Your Own Career Path, gives you advice about what to do now, identifies helpful reading materials and Web sites, and lists organizations you may contact for additional information. As you think about a career in engineering, consider these ideas:

- As you go through your day, try to identify all the individual technologies that you use or are used to help you in your day. Think about the engineer who designed, created, or maintained these technologies.
- Take advantage of engineering exploration days at local companies—if you know an engineer, ask to shadow her at work one day so you can see the jobs she does.
- As soon as you can, take chemistry, algebra, biology, and courses that help you understand how the world works.
- Identify a role model or mentor and work with her as you prepare for your career.
- Test the waters early! Many companies have programs for student internships immediately after high school graduation. Some summer "camps" introduce engineering. Talk to your parents and guidance counselor about local vocational guidance programs in your area; talk to adult engineers to see if their companies have programs, and investigate federal- or state-funded internship programs.

## Changing the World

Today, women can be found in all the engineering professions. Women are becoming heads of major corporations, are leading research labs, and are investigating cuttingedge ways to develop new technologies. Like me, women engineers can serve at high levels of the government and are members of the National Academy of Engineering, an honorary society of some of the most innovative and creative engineers in the United States. An engineering career takes time, education, and a willingness to help people. If you enjoy finding out how things work, solving problems or puzzles, creating and building, and looking forward to the future, then perhaps an engineering career is for you. The most important reason to choose engineering should be your desire to make a difference.

## What Are Engineering Fields?
## Aerospace Engineering

*Aero* relates to aircraft. Engineers work with the design, development, testing, and production of aircraft, also missiles, space vehicles, and underwater vehicles. Aerospace engineering is an outgrowth of aeronautics (science of flight) and includes astronautics (travel beyond earth's atmosphere). Engineers also help solve problems caused by these methods of transportation, like noise pollution.

## Bioengineering

*Bio* refers to living organisms, including human beings. Bioengineers solve problems related to biological systems (like purification of water) and human health. Engineers design and develop processes and improve equipment like lasers for surgery, artificial organs, and monitoring equipment. Biomedical engineers do clinical research on such things as genetics and skin adaptation to prostheses.

## Chemical Engineering

Chemists develop processes and products, then chemical engineers figure out how to produce them on a large scale, safely and efficiently. They are concerned that these processes don't pollute the air, water, or land. Engineers improve chemical processes, design equipment like large reactors, refineries, or safety systems, oversee construction, and improve operations. One speciality is plastics.

## Civil Engineering

The word *civil* relates to the general public. Civil engineers work on such projects as bridges, buildings, and highways, things the public uses. They design, research, supervise construction, and are concerned with problems like air, noise, water pollution, floods, and earthquakes.

## Computer Science and Engineering

Engineers work with computer software, databases, artificial intelligence, robotics, networking, and design software.

## Electric Power/Energy Systems Engineering

These engineers work with the systems that generate large amounts of power, like your local power company, and large dams that generate power. They are concerned with the effective and safe use of energy and its interactions with the environment.

## Electronic Engineering

These engineers work with the systems that generate small amounts of power, like telephones, computers, radar, television, radio, cellular phones, and satellite communication systems. They design and improve systems and solve communication problems.

## Industrial, Manufacturing, and Operational Systems Engineering

Think of the wide variety of products manufactured, from automobiles to xylophones. Engineers are involved in the planning, management, and operation of the manufacturing process from raw material to the finished product, including design of the product, the equipment, and the layout of the plant. They often are concerned with recycling and safe management of resources.

## Materials Engineering

These engineers focus on the properties of the material being used, its relation to such things as heat, and its strengths and weaknesses for the particular purpose. They want to be sure materials perform safely and efficiently and to their most useful purpose. One of the specialties is ceramics.

## Mechanical Engineering

Mechanical engineers work with machines and tools that produce, transmit, or use power. These can be huge gears or delicate instruments. Some areas are air conditioning, elevators, printing presses, nuclear reactors, aircraft engines. Their work also includes air pollution control and environmental systems.

## Petroleum, Mining, and Geological Engineering

Here the knowledge and problem-solving skills apply to the mineral and energy resources within the earth—exploring, processing raw material, storing it in a safe and efficient way, including concerns for clean environment.

## Special Fields

Special fields of engineering are specialities people go into after advanced studies. As people apply engineering principles to solve new problems, these areas will change and grow. Here are some of the special fields you may have heard about: acoustics, agriculture, environmental, geothermal, hydrological, military, molecular, ocean, optical, transportation.

The 12 broad categories above, as organized by the National Academy of Engineering, represent the disciplines of engineering practiced by the individual members and foreign associates of the NAE. The NAE is an honorary organization of outstanding engineers that serves the nation by providing advice to the U.S. Government about matters concerning engineering and technology.

# COOL
## careers
### for
## girls

## in
# ENGINEERING

Credit: Lloyd Dennis Photography

# Lisa Harmon

**Owner/President,** L'Acquis Consulting Enterprises, Inc.
(doing business as LACE Consulting Engineers), New Orleans, LA

Major in Mechanical Engineering

# Mechanical Engineer, Entrepreneur

## Quality Designs for City Businesses

When Lisa Harmon gets to her office at 8:00 a.m. on a Monday, her first effort is to check the status of the company's active design engineering projects. Are there any problems delaying work on the projects? Is equipment working well? How are the designs coming? When will the blueprints drawn on the computer be ready to look at? Does she need to check the cost estimate or schedule a meeting with a client? Do any of her 19 employees need to meet with her?

The next effort is to see if the proposals for new clients are ready. Then she checks on projects under construction. As Lisa answers all of these

# LISA'S CAREER PATH

**Plays Piano** at 5,
▼ starts singing in choirs
at 9 years old,

**Likes** math, art,
▼ Star Trek's Scotty

**Graduates**
▼ college

questions, she schedules the company's work for the coming week and gives employees work assignments. LACE Consulting Engineers does a lot of work with air conditioning systems—new buildings with new systems or repairing and reengineering systems in older buildings to improve the air quality and make sure it meets new standards set by the federal and state governments. The company's projects also include work on plumbing systems, water treatment plants, chemical plants, and other industrial sites. Lisa's engineers design electrical systems, sprinkler systems, fire alarms, and other safety devices. "We recently did several exhaust hoods for commercial kitchens. The hoods contained a complex system of chemicals that would help put out any type of cooking fire."

When Lisa plans new projects, she estimates how many hours of work a new project will take, creates a proposal, and schedules a meeting to sit down with the customer and explain the details. Most of her projects come to her first as an RFP (request for proposal). A company or a branch of the city or state government requests proposals from design firms, giving details on what they would like done. For example, a school might need a new air conditioning system designed. The designers prepare bid documents which detail and specify the work to be done. Then contractors propose, in a bid, how much it would cost and how long it would take.

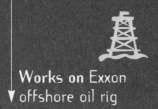

# A Double
# Minority Business

Lisa is able to bid on some jobs because her business fits into a minority category. "I'm a 'double minority' as a woman-owned and African-American-owned business." Government regulations require businesses to offer equal opportunities to contractors. Therefore, Lisa must match the "type of business" requirements listed on RFPs. Minority businesses don't automatically get the jobs, though. They have to be competitive with all of the others bidding for the job and have a reputation for delivering quality work.

A native of New Orleans, Louisiana,

Lisa has 22 years of experience in mechanical engineering. She has owned her own business since 1987. "It was hard when I first started," says Lisa. "I had to learn about marketing my services. I had to learn how the RFPs were drawn up and all the politics of

Credit: Lloyd Dennis Photography

getting your bid seriously considered. At first there was a suspicion that I was just a 'front,' that I didn't really

9

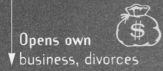
own the business and didn't do any of the work. I had to market my know-how and my skills from my previous work experience—sell myself, which was difficult for me." It took about six months before Lisa got the first pro-

were supportive, but nobody else among my friends had done what I was trying to do."

After a hectic period of hiring helpers and then letting them go because they just didn't work out, Lisa

> ## I had to market my know-how and my skills from my previous work experience—sell myself, which was difficult for me.

ject for her business. It took about a year and one half to overcome the "just a front" suspicions.

"I know what I can do and what I can't do. When people thought I might not be capable, that just made me more determined. I wanted to prove them wrong. My friends and family

met a woman mechanical engineer who, with her husband, had defected from Poland and moved to New Orleans, but had trouble getting engineering work because of language problems. She had the skills Lisa needed. They worked together to build LACE, Inc., for three years be-

10

fore she moved out of the area. Now Lisa employs two electrical engineers, two mechanical engineers, one civil engineer, and one licensed surveyor in addition to a support staff of 10.

One of her company's recent projects was to modify a street car barn (used to house the New Orleans street cars) and add a spray paint booth. The booth had to have good lighting, an air vacuuming system to pull the paint in the air away from the people doing the painting, and a heat system to help dry the paint. "We also designed a dust collection system in the carpentry shop to automatically vacuum up the dust from the cutting and sanding operations."

Lisa also does asbestos abatement design, which sometimes requires that she put on a "TyVek" suit, which covers her from head to foot like an astronaut's space suit. She wears a respirator and checks for asbestos, which is a harmful substance.

## CAREER CHECKLIST

You'll like this job if you ...

Like mathematics

Are not easily discouraged

Are a good judge of people

Have a positive attitude

Have a work ethic, are self-motivated

Will learn what you need to know

# JOB FACTS

**HOURS:** 8:00 a.m. to 6:00 or 6:30 p.m.

**OFFICE:** Has her own office with a door and window

**CLOTHES:** Business clothes. Keeps a pair of jeans, safety work shoes, and a hard hat in her office so she can change if she visits a work site.

**DUTIES:** Runs own business—administration, marketing, quality control, and people management. Experienced in engineering design and writing proposals to bid on a variety of projects that require air conditioning, plumbing, fire protection, electrical power distribution, lighting, surveying, and asbestos abatement.

**$ALARY:** People who start their own business may not earn any salary in the beginning. They invest their own money in the business, they get more money through loans or venture capital, and, until they make a profit or "go public" by selling stock, they probably pay themselves a small salary and put profits back into the business to help it grow. Sometimes when they sell the business, they sign a contract that pays them executive compensation to stay and manage the company.

# A Song in Her Heart

Credit: Lloyd Dennis Photography

When Lisa was a girl, she first wanted to be a doctor. Then she got interested in outer space and the U.S. space program. She is still a big fan of Star Trek's famous engineer, Scotty. "Scotty always managed to fix things. I love that." While she was good at math in school, she also liked art, especially drawing. One constant in her life is music. Lisa started playing the piano when she was 5 years old. She studied piano for 10 years, then took up the flute to be in the high school symphonic and marching bands. Lisa started singing in choirs when she was in the fourth grade and has been in a choir ever since.

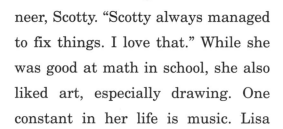

[ When people thought I might not be capable, that just made me more determined. ]

Lisa's mom and dad expected her to be a doctor, but when Lisa got to college she decided to major in mechanical engineering. "I could see how creative engineering was, and I liked that. I really enjoyed the casual dress code of wearing jeans to class after the emphasis on clothes in high school. My tomboy nature came out, maybe because we were just 6 women in a

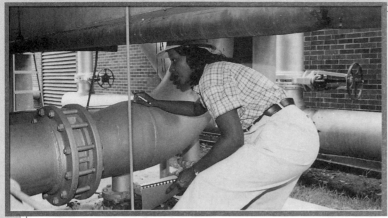

Credit: Lloyd Dennis Photography

class of 50 men." Lisa also took dance and kept up with her choir and group singing, though there was little leisure time with her schedule of 18 to 21 credit hours per semester.

When it came time to seek a job, Lisa had offers from companies in Delaware, Texas, Tennessee, and at home in Louisiana. "I visited Tennessee to explore a job in nuclear energy, which sounded real interesting. But I didn't like the town or the food. I took a New Orleans job with Exxon, which also paid the most money."

# Offshore Rigs & Chemical Plants

At the oil company Exxon, Lisa's projects were varied. She worked in the Subsurface Engineering Group and the Inland Drilling Group. Several times Lisa would travel by helicopter then by boat out to an offshore drilling platform to do repair work. "It was fun. I would do the work, write it up, stay overnight, and return."

Lisa learned a lot in her three years with Exxon, but got bored doing the same type of projects and wanted to try something different. Through contacts with friends, she learned about a firm called W. S. Nelson Co. and contacted them about a job. "I worked for Nelson for eight years. They encouraged me to continue learning, and supported me in getting my PE (professional engineering certification). The work was multifaceted, interesting, and challenging."

Lisa worked with teams of engineers to design offshore platforms, modify chemical plants, and do municipal engineering. "The work gave me a chance to apply the sciences I studied. It's not like art; it is concrete, but it's creative, making things work efficiently."

One of her favorite projects was the design and construction of a particleboard plant, which involved pneumatic conveying, and "cooking, pressing, and cutting" the product.

During this time, Lisa met and married her first husband, and her daughter, Yvahn, was born. "It was hard going back to work after my maternity leave. I was determined to stick with it, though I wished the idea of flextime had been more acceptable then."

uncertain, she began preparing herself to open her own business.

As Lisa pioneered her new business, she and her husband grew apart. They decided to separate, and later they divorced. Lisa had met Richard Harmon, a mechanical engineer, when she was visiting one of her job sites. They discovered they had mutual friends and had seen each other occasionally over the years. Later they began dating and are now married. Today, Richard helps Lisa run the business. Even though her

# Learn your interests, talents, and limitations, but don't limit yourself.

But things changed when a mild depression caused a slowdown in industrial projects, and Nelson Consulting began to seek commercial and government agency work. That's when Lisa learned about the advantages a woman-owned, African-American-owned business would receive. With her future at Nelson

business can be demanding and time consuming, Lisa makes time for her family, friends, church, and singing.

# Heidi Bauer

**Software Engineer**, Macromedia, Inc., Redwood Shores, CA

Major in Computer Science

# Computer
## Engineer

## Web Tool Designer

Heidi Bauer is the only woman on a team of 13 software engineers. She says what she loves best about her job is that she's working with the most talented and fabulous engineers she has ever met. "They aren't macho at all, and the team is an easy and comfortable place for me."

Heidi works in Redwood Shores, California, about half an hour south of San Francisco, for a company called Macromedia. Her second favorite thing about her job is that she gets to work on a very creative software product—Dreamweaver—that helps people make amazing designs on the World Wide Web. "I think computer programming is a creative process, more of an art than a science. It is problem solving and logic and really putting creative, interesting user interfaces on things."

Heidi had worked at Macromedia as an intern and took a full-time position there after college. After only eight months, she became a software engineer for the Dreamweaver project. The first visual Web-authoring tool of its kind, Dreamweaver allows the user to visually edit a page on the Web and also to have "fine" control of HTML, a coding language used to create Web pages. "It is rare that you will have the opportunity to build a brand new software tool (there is nothing in the world like it yet)."

## Writing Code

When Heidi started with the company in the Spring of 1996, her job was to write the software "code" for "plugins" that would work with all the company's products. Plugins are pieces of code that extend an application's functionality beyond what was originally written. For example, every Macromedia product has to know how to "render" images that are in different formats, such as JPEG or GIF files. Heidi wrote code to tell the software how to ask for the specifics of the image—height and width and actual color bits. She helped create the software "architecture" that would allow the tool to speak to other pieces of code to get this information. After the plugin was written once, each Macromedia product could use it to render its images.

Heidi's manager at the time came up with the idea for Dreamweaver. When he was named to direct the team that would build it, he asked Heidi if she wanted to work on the project. "He reminded me that it's bet-

18

Studies computer
science in college

Spends 3 months at
outdoor leadership
school in Mexico

Gets internship,
graduates college

ter to work on projects that will generate revenue than doing what I was doing, which was basically a nonrevenue-generating project."

"I was one of the junior engineers on

did a lot of the implementation to support it."

Layering is a new part of HTML. The first version of HTML was very static. Once you loaded a page into the

## My life's motto is: I'll keep doing what I'm doing until I stop having fun.

the team when I first started on Dreamweaver, and a lot of other people had way more software engineering experience than I did. I was paired with another engineer. Together we worked on the features that would allow the user to create and use HTML layers. He did a lot of the big, sweeping architectural work, and I

Web browser, the initial content was all you could get. But new technology allows for layering. The person who builds the Web page can overlap the content in different layers. The person who is writing the Web page can use Java Script to animate the layers and have things fly across the page, appear, and disappear.

The longer Heidi was on the team, the more code she worked on. Eventually, she began doing everything from designing code to actually implementing codes as a part of the software tool. She also has become known as an engineer who can be given any piece of code in Dreamweaver and figure out exactly how it works. She can find the bugs in the code and fix them pretty fast. In this way, she has assumed lots of responsibility for knowing how the whole product works, not just for the pieces she has worked on.

Dreamweaver is used by Web designers who run their own Web design studios and also by people who work on a company's Intranet (a network like the Internet only protected by "fire walls" so that only people who work at the company can see the information).

## How It All Starts

There is a certain cycle a software team must develop when creating new versions. For Dreamweaver, that cycle begins with customer research. This includes traveling to different customer sites. (Engineers on Heidi's team went to Seattle, Los Angeles, Boston, Chicago, and New York to talk to customers.) It also includes checking the emails from the Dreamweaver newsgroup (customers) to see what they are having trouble with or what they especially like. The team also checks on any new HTML standards.

When Heidi and her teammates have a list of features they think would be good to put into a new version of the software, they evaluate the list to see which features are practical. That means they have to consider how much time it would take to create a new feature (and whether the competition could come out with a better product before they finished). They work with other engineers in the company, as well as the marketing department, to decide on the new features, and then, how to present these features so that it is evident that the new product is far superior to the previous version. The trick is to decide on those features that customers want but which won't take so long to build that the product will be out of date before it is ready for sale.

One improvement in one of the versions of Dreamweaver lets the user

# CAREER CHECKLIST

## You'll like this job if you ...

Are independent and curious

Are willing to ask lots of questions

Know how to use your voice to speak up and make your opinion known

Like to be on the cutting edge of ideas and technology

Love to figure out how to make creative things

Like to work with others and on your own

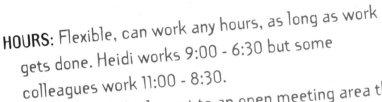

# ON THE JOB

**HOURS:** Flexible, can work any hours, as long as work gets done. Heidi works 9:00 - 6:30 but some colleagues work 11:00 - 8:30.

**WORKPLACE:** Cubicle next to an open meeting area that contains comfortable, fuzzy, blue and red furniture with big purple and green polkadot rug. Lots of light and windows.

**CLOTHES:** Very casual. Dress-up Fridays—engineers dress for a theme such as red for Valentine's Day or green for St. Patrick's Day or 1980s clothing.

**DUTIES:** Research on the computer to see what's happening with Web technology, visits to customers to see what they like or don't like about the software, writing code in C+, C++, HTML, JavaScript, Visual C++, Code Warrior. Fixing bugs in the software. Evaluating new features for new versions.

**$ALARY:** $60,000 to $75,000 and up.

launch a graphics tool right from Dreamweaver rather than having to switch back and forth between the graphics tool and Dreamweaver.

Once the features have been decided on, the team sits down and draws how the new product will work and how it should be designed. Then the product is designed and tested by the quality assurance engineers to find and fix any bugs. When the product is ready to be tested on the public, some customers get to put it on their system. This is called a beta test. Customers give the Dreamweaver team feedback on how they like the product and how it runs. Then any bugs that haven't yet been fixed get fixed. Once the bugs are fixed and the product ships, the team gets a well-deserved vacation. Then they come back and start on a new cycle for the next version.

# Not Bored at Boarding School

Heidi had no idea until she was a sophomore in college that she would end up working in the computer industry. Her father was a mechanical engineer and as a girl she had tinkered with cars and been interested in mechanical things. She grew up in the northwest part of Vermont, not far from the Canadian border, in a town of about 3,000. Her mother was a nurse who worked in home health care.

When it came time for high school, Heidi's parents thought it would be better if she went to a boarding school to prepare to get into a good college. Both Heidi and her brother, who is a year older than she, went to boarding schools. "We were given a choice of five or six schools, and I chose a school in Concord, Massachusetts, just outside Boston. Most of the kids there came from much bigger cities than I did, so it was a little intimidating at first, but once I got used to it, I loved it there."

Heidi's day at boarding school began at 7:00 a.m. and ended at about 10:00 p.m., including time spent in classes, studying, and playing sports. The school had about 300 kids, half boys and half girls. Heidi played baseball (on an all-boy team), basketball, and soccer; she took dance classes and rowed on the crew team. On holidays, she went home to Vermont.

## Discovering Programming Was Great

After high school Heidi went to Brown University, where she planned to study education, psychology, anthropology, or languages. She thought science was boring and dull. But she was dating someone who was majoring in computer science, and he kept telling her how much fun it was. Between her freshman and sophomore years, Heidi took an aptitude test given by the Johnson-O'Connor Research Foundation that suggested one of the things she would enjoy was computer pro-gramming. The next year she took her first computer science class.

"I knew right then I definitely would major in computer science," Heidi says. "I absolutely loved the course. But I still wasn't sure whether I would like working in the computer industry."

Heidi's first course was an introduction to programming using object-oriented PASCAL as the programming language. The course taught the basic programming concepts, functions, and parameters. Heidi learned that even with basic computer knowledge it was possible to put together complex programs that could do interesting things. Her last project was to write a game of Othello for the computer. "After that I started taking as many computer courses as I could."

> You have to be willing to ask questions if you don't know how something works or don't know what's going on. You also have to be proactive in learning the code if you don't already know it.

"It was completely accidental that I got into computers at all. When I was in my junior year of high school I went through all the math classes, all the way through calculus. Then I got to take 'Math 9,' which was discrete mathematics. It basically was about logic, which is the basis for a lot of computer science. I argued with the teacher that this course was about computers, and we were supposed to be taking math classes. I yelled at him that it was ridiculous that we had to take the course. A couple of years later I went back and told him I was sorry that I hadn't understood the value of that class better, and he said they had taken it off the curriculum. A lot of students had complained. It wasn't until I had a college level course in discrete mathematics that I saw the link, and saw how valuable that subject is."

In college, Heidi took anthropology, French, and writing classes in addition to her computer science. She still likes to write, and she loves to read. In the middle of her junior year, she took three months off to attend the National Outdoor Leadership School. She and 15 strangers spent three months in Baja, Mexico, learning rock climbing, spear fishing, hiking, and sailing. "This experience gave me the self-confidence I have today," Heidi says. "It taught me good survival skills. If I could do that, I could do anything."

In her spare time, Heidi keeps up with her soccer. She has recently joined a team in the Golden Gate Women's Soccer League, and plays ten games per season with two seasons a year. She also loves to kayak and ski with her boyfriend on weekends.

# Karen Thomas

Karen Thomas

**Team Leader,** Process Section, General Engineering Department, Texaco, Inc., Houston, TX

Major in Chemical Engineering; master's degree in Chemical Engineering

# Chemical Engineer

## From Oil Rigs to Reactors

**K**aren Thomas is a chemical engineer with the oil company Texaco. She has worked in research, helped design a unique process, and been part of a project that resulted in construction of a new plant. That plant is safely and efficiently producing new chemical products. "I still feel excited when I drive down the road and see that plant, making money for the company, creating jobs for people."

## First-of-a-kind

Karen joined Texaco as a senior engineer in Houston, Texas. Her first five months she spent in research, joining a team whose mission was to create a new process (resulting in new products for Texaco). Over a period of four years, Karen worked with other engineers, outside consultants, and contractors to design a first-of-a-kind process, then test its operation. She traveled to Germany and the Netherlands to talk to people about the project. Because of her work, which was design of the reactor area, Karen is co-owner of the patent. (The reactor is Many companies buy this product to use in making such consumer products as shampoo or car parts or insulation.) During the final stages of the project, Karen was named "process lead," to lead members of the overall design support team.

> For chemical engineers, there is a wide variety of things you can do. You can work in research, in plant operations, in design, and in management. You can work in oil refineries, chemical plants, food, and other manufacturing environments.

like a big pressure cooker. Its contents enter from separate pipes, then mix and react under pressure, and in this case, the reaction results in creating the new product Propylene Oxide. "We used computer modeling of the large scale reactor to test it for safety. We would input the physical properties: the quantities, chemical concentrations, and temperatures and then

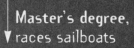 
Master's degree,
races sailboats

Development
engineer, gets
first patent

Moves to Texas,
meets Charles

test the reactions. We designed controls, alarms, backup systems, and shut-off safety measures."

It is a difficult job to take the small pilot plant reactor and move it up to a real-life, large-scale reactor, so the design team must solve the problems before construction can start. Once construction starts, the tech-support team takes over to coordinate the work, review drawings, answer questions, and solve problems that come up. That's why Karen, as leader of that team, lived near the site several months during actual construction and startup of the $500 million plant's operation.

## Creative Problem Solving

Now Karen acts as a consultant to the operating plant, which is in East Texas, but she usually stays in Houston and solves problems through telephone conversations. Her main job is to be one of three team leaders in the process design group for Texaco's central engineering group. Since the oil company has plants around the world, the engineers are concerned

with global operations. "We try to find new solutions to old problems, conceive new processes and new ways to use equipment—like offshore platform design for oil rigs. We look at current research to see if we can put it into practice (like making gasoline from natural gas) and move it into the real world in a practical, environmentally safe, and economical way."

Karen supervises about 15 engineers. She enjoys the administrative and management activities. "I get a charge out of helping people who work for me. I want to make their

assignments a win/win for them and the company. I also see that their training is helpful and appropriate and that their travel is as convenient as possible."

Karen also helps recruit engineers for Texaco's central engineering group and is especially involved with the intern program. "We have four interns in our group each summer. They help the engineers on projects, and we try to give them interesting work. They also have activities with the other interns in the company-wide program. My intern experience before my senior year in college was a good one, and I think it is important to provide worthwhile experience to these students. We hire some of the interns when they finish school."

## Her Father's Influence

Karen grew up in small towns in Kentucky. Her father, a civil engineer, worked on big projects like dam construction. "I always thought of my dad as very capable, doing important things. There was tremendous activity, huge equipment to see, and I tagged along when he gave family and friends tours of the dam. He was the resident engineer in charge of construction, so we lived there during construction."

When Karen was 14, her father was transferred to the district office of the U.S. Army Corps of Engineers, and the family moved to Nashville. "I was in eighth grade, and it was a big adjustment, to live in a big city."

"I would never have thought of being an engineer back then (in the 1970s) if my father hadn't been one,"

# CAREER CHECKLIST ✓

## You'll like this job if you ...

- Want to keep getting better at things
- Can think creatively
- Can work on a team or alone
- Can be focused and patient
- Enjoy big challenges
- Can use and remember important facts and details
- Are interested in computer modeling

# JOB FACTS

**HOURS:** When in the office, business hours—8:30 to 5:00. When in the field on a project, various and long hours for several days—7:00 to 4:00 at plant, then several hours in testing lab, then meetings with team members

**WORKPLACE:** Office cubicle, chemical plant, oil refinery, drilling platform

**CLOTHES:** Business suit, overalls, work shoes, safety gear (hard hat, goggles, safety harness)

**DUTIES:** Find new solutions to problems, think up new processes and new ways to use equipment (like offshore platform design for oil rigs), review current research to see if it can be put into practical use, and supervise 15 engineers

**$ALARY:** Chemical Engineer
Starting salary $36,700 to $41,700

says Karen. "My mother was in social work but loved math, so I probably inherited some math and problem-solving skills from both of them. My parents never steered me toward engineering, but they were supportive and told me I could be anything I wanted to be. My younger sister is also an engineer."

In high school, besides being good in math and science, Karen played clarinet in the marching band. "When it came time to go to college, I chose Auburn University because they had good programs in the two areas I was thinking about studying—architecture and engineering. They also had a good marching band."

The summer before her senior year, Karen worked as an engineering intern for Dow Chemical in Plaquemine, Louisiana. "My professor advisor helped me get the position. It was in research, but the complex had 2,000 employees, and I got to go on tours and see different areas, including several operating plants and the plant design group. I was actually responsible for

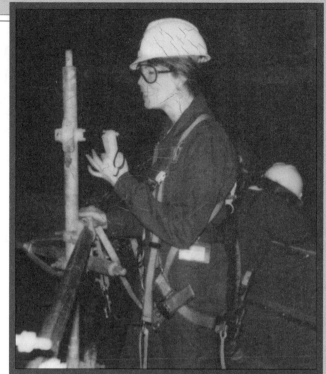

day-to-day stuff in the pilot plant." That experience convinced Karen that she wanted to become a chemical engineer and eventually work in the creative area of design—working on new processes, developing new ways of doing things, not just improving current processes.

For advanced study, Karen chose the University of Florida at Gainesville because it had a good graduate chemical engineering department and its master's program was theoretical, which was different from her practical studies at Auburn. As part of her master's thesis, she developed a computer simulation to model various stages of conversion of water hyacinths (the floating aquatic plant that often clogs waterways in the South) to methane gas, for the Gas Research Institute.

After she got her master's degree in

tion. The new process produced a higher quality product per month at a lower cost than the previous process.

"I liked my job, but I wasn't sure if I wanted to stay in research and development. I also wanted to quit renting and buy a house. So I went on inter-

[
# By working on improving my speaking and presentation skills, I've gotten opportunities I might not otherwise have had.
]

chemical engineering, Karen worked in northern Florida at Olin Corporation as a development engineer in process research. One example of her work: she developed a method for relating raw material properties (such as reaction to temperature) to processing problems. This led her to develop (like an inventor does) and patent an uninterrupted continuous process that replaced a "batch" opera-

views. The reason I had chosen chemical engineering over other types of engineering was the variety of work. I wanted to see what jobs were out there."

## Confidence with Toastmasters

When Karen entered the world of work at Olin, she realized that she had to conquer her fear of speaking before a group. She knew she'd have to "present" her work results to others. She also knew that it would help her career and get her noticed if she did it well. "I was absolutely petrified, and I knew I had to turn that around. I joined Toastmasters. They were so

supportive. I was able to stumble, 'fall on my face' before that group and get feedback on how to improve. When the time came to give a presentation at work, I managed and even received some compliments."

While in Florida, Karen learned to sail a Hobie Catamaran, a small sailboat with two hulls connected by a "deck" of canvas.

When she's not working, speaking, or racing her Hobie, Karen Thomas Barnett enjoys married life with Charles. They especially like to travel together to new, out-of-the-way places and went to Argentina for their honeymoon. They both had their own homes when they married in 1997, so they decided to sell those houses and buy "their own home." Of course, there has to be room for the sailing gear and the Hobie Cat.

Credit: Kevin Weber Photography

# Joan Sanders

Joan Sanders

**Associate Professor,** University of Washington, Seattle, WA

Major in Mechanical Engineering, master's degree in Mechanical Engineering,
Ph.D. degree in Bioengineering

# Biomedical Engineer, Researcher

## Engineering Patient Comfort

When Joan Sanders was getting her master's degree in mechanical engineering, she looked for courses that would teach her how to combine her engineering knowledge with applications in medicine, but she could only find two. She got frustrated because the courses she wanted didn't exist. That was back in the mid 1980s, before biomedical engineering became a recognized field for research with its own academic standards and career track. Eventually, Joan realized that, just because very few people had synthesized medical and engineering knowledge into a field of study, it didn't mean she couldn't make a career out of it.

"I realized that what I wanted to do

# JOAN'S CAREER PATH

Plays sports in school

Graduates college

Works at hospitals, observes patients with prostheses

was not going on in the field and that it was okay to create a new field and work in it to solve clinical problems. That was a big change for me—realizing that if the path wasn't there I could create it myself."

to produce results that will allow the manufacturers of artificial limbs (prostheses) to enhance the quality of wearers' lives. Joan's three main areas of research are prosthetic engineering (making artificial limbs fit

> Take all the lab courses you can—physics, chemistry, things that require experiments. Also learn to think logically. I did this by having to write term papers that were clear and logical.

Today Joan specializes in research that uses the principles of engineering to create solutions for medical problems. Right now, Joan is working

better and be more comfortable for people who need to wear them), biomaterials (finding out what materials work best for human skin of a pros-

thesis wearer whose skin is damaged or burned), and skin adaptation (finding how skin naturally adjusts to become more load tolerant—like the bottom of the feet in jogging—so that molecular engineering can be used to design medicines to make the skin more trauma resistant for patients).

## Settled in Seattle

Joan works at the University of Washington, where she earned her Ph.D. It's unusual, but for Joan, it's a good arrangement to stay at the university where she did her doctoral research. For the school, it's a benefit to have Joan run the prosthetic engineering and related research program. She has been quite successful in bringing large research grants (funding) to the university, and her work is well-known and appreciated by people in the biomedical engineering and health care fields.

Joan's latest grant is for $2 million from the National Center for Medical Rehabilitation Research in the National Institutes of Health, a U.S. government agency under the Depart. of Health and Human Services. Joan and the 25 researchers in her laboratory will use the money to determine the optimum size and the shape-adjustment process for a made-to-order fit. That will require

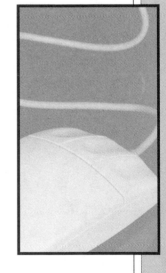

clinical measurements and computer modeling to determine the pressures and shear stresses that occur at the point where an artificial leg meets the human limb. With the correct information about pressures and shear stresses, socket shape adjustment systems can be designed to disburse the stress from the body over a wide area, so the prosthesis not only will be more comfortable to wear, but will also fit better.

The way prostheses are designed today makes it common for the wearer to have a tight fit in the morning and a very loose fit at night, because the body fluid shifts during the day. One of the consequences of this shifting and the ensuing bad fit is that the skin gets rubbed and irritated. While this might not sound serious, it can be devastating to the wearer, who has to be in a wheelchair or on crutches if the skin develops a sore and the prosthesis can't be worn.

The researchers want to find a drug that can be applied topically to strengthen the skin, so it won't develop sores. Joan says they already know that the skin reacts locally—that is, alone. The circulatory system and nervous system aren't involved in the primary adaptations the skin makes to the prosthesis. That's good news because it means the changes

Credit: Kevin Weber Photography

are limited to the skin and not complicated by the functions of other organs in the body.

# Practical but
## Broad Research

"It's unusual to have a program that combines the practical work of prosthetics research with the technical research on biomaterials and the very technical research on the skin," Joan says. "That's the strength of our group—that our research is so broad."

Joan got interested in skin research because she wanted to solve the problems that came when the patients used their prostheses. As she spent more time with patients, she saw that the way the skin reacted was a huge problem for them. That led to her interest in trying to "engineer" the skin, which led to an interest in skin adaptation and understanding the physiology of the skin. "It's very exciting," she says. "We are the only ones doing skin adaptation research. Most people tend to look at wound healing, but by then it's too late. The patient has already been deprived of use of the

# CAREER CHECKLIST ✔

## You'll like this job if you ...

Can sell your ideas to get the grants you will need

Have tenacity; won't get discouraged and give up

Like math and physics

Are fascinated with how things work

Like to build mechanical things

Can solve problems creatively

Love to use your imagination to think about how to make things better

Want to help people have higher quality lives

# JOB FACTS

**HOURS:** 65 to 70 hours per week, usually 8:00 a.m. to 7:00 p.m., six days a week

**WORKPLACE:** Laboratory, office for consulting and counseling, classroom

**CLOTHES:** Business clothes, laboratory coat

**DUTIES:** Sets priorities for research laboratory and supervises researchers. Advises students. Teaches biomedical engineering classes. Writes grant proposals.

**$ALARIES:**

Research assistant professor starting salary $54,000

Associate professor average $75,000

Consultant $150 per hour

Starting salary for biomedical engineer $30,000

Average salary $40,000 to $55,000

Credit: Kevin Weber Photography

limb. We want to engineer the skin before the breakdown occurs, which is an extremely novel idea in the field."

When Joan joined the University of Washington faculty, she was hired in a problem to solve. Every patient is different and every situation presents us with new challenges."

For Joan, one of the best parts of her job is advising the students who have

> Don't be afraid to contact professors you admire. Keep sending them emails until they respond to you. The surest way to get their attention is to go to the library and read what they have written and then go to them with questions about their work.

research track position, doing research all day. After a year of successful grant proposals, she accepted the university's offer of a tenured track position. "That's much better. It pays most of my salary, I have a large amount of laboratory space, and I do a lot of teaching." Joan likes to teach because she is always learning as she teaches her students. "We go to the OR (operating room) or talk to the patients and see what doesn't work and try to figure out why. That gives us a chosen to do research in her laboratory. The competition to get into her program is very tough. She also teaches one class a quarter, about three hours of lectures a week. In addition, Joan has to supervise the full-time laboratory employees who aren't students.

Joan enjoys working with the undergraduates the most. They are enthusiastic and full of ideas. With graduate students, Joan advises them on the scientific quality and world-wide opportunities for their research, but the students choose the project. With undergraduates, she provides more direction, depending on the interest and skill level of the student. "It's fun to see the transition from somebody coming in and saying what should I be doing, to the person who says, okay, here's what I think we should do to solve this problem."

Students come from all over the school, not just the bioengineering program, to work with Joan. "This works really well. Each student has an area of expertise, and they are very competitive, but they realize they need to understand what each of the others is doing and help to get the whole project done. This is the same thing that is happening in industry. The individual researcher or scientist is a thing of the past. You have to be able to work with others and open up your mind to other perspectives. You have to pay attention and ask good questions and try to understand as much about the other discipline as you can."

## A National Agenda

Another part of the job that Joan loves is talking to people at the National Institutes of Health, legislative policymakers, professional scientific societies, and other scientists about policy and research directions for biomedical engineering. She has served on recommendation committees, as well as a number of scientific review panels. "It helps to set a national agenda or direction. It's rewarding because these people listen to what I have to say. Bioengineering is such a

hot issue in this country right now. We want to be sure that we set the direction so there is tremendous opportunity for research, and we don't lose the focus on cross-functional work (different disciplines working together). You take mechanical engineers and you introduce them to bioengineering (which is the global term for this field, biomedical engineering refers specifically to research with a clinical emphasis). Sometimes they get it and sometimes they don't. The reason they may not get it is that they aren't used to opening up their minds and allowing for the 'gray fuzziness' of medicine. If you go to a clinic and listen to a doctor who is with a patient for 10 minutes, you will see the doctor take a few simple measurements and then say, 'here's what your problem is.' That's totally different from what an engineer does. The engineer has to write all these equations and do all this analysis. The doctor doesn't have charts and graphs to back up her judgments, but her experience will tell her this is probably what is happening. The doctor is the knowledge base, and engineers need to take some of their cues from her. We also need to take basic research from cell biology and

similar fields and apply it to real life situations."

"Biomedical engineering departments are typically divided into pathways—biomechanics, imaging, cellular systems. The students say the faculty fit into the pathways, but the students themselves aren't interested in the pathways. They are between faculty, so to speak. They will take a new technology and combine it with another new technology or an older one, to create a new field. So we are creating a student who is a new breed. Just think, molecular engineering didn't even exist eight years ago. Pioneering bioengineers said, 'we will engineer proteins at the molecular level' and they created the field!"

# Wanted Less Pain, More Gain

Joan grew up in Los Angeles, the daughter of an electrical engineer. In high school and college she was very athletic and played all types of sports. "When you do a lot of sports you get hurt a lot. I became interested in how I could improve my performance so I wouldn't get hurt so much. That's where my interest in mechanics and engineering started. I wanted to know how the muscles worked and how I could get them to work better."

Joan's parents encouraged her to do whatever she was interested in. It did not matter if she were better at sports than her brothers or if her interests weren't considered feminine. She loved taking things apart and putting them back together and building little machines, like a car that could go downhill sideways. She liked building rockets and experimenting with the concepts of trajectory and speed.

When she got to college, Joan wanted to be a professional athlete. But shortly into her college studies at Stanford University in Palo Alto, California, she realized that probably wouldn't be possible, because very few

Credit: Kevin Weber Photography

sports were available to women and the competition was so tough. So she declared a mechanical engineering major. She began interacting with sports medicine people and got jobs at hospitals, where she could see how broken bones and other ailments got fixed. She read everything she could about the emerging field of bioengineering.

While working on her master's degree in mechanical engineering at Northwestern University in Chicago, Illinois, one of Joan's projects was to figure out why high pressure needleless syringes left bruises or damaged a muscle on the recipients and why they often just didn't work. Joan and her research partners discovered that the explosion from the syringe gun caused a series of pressure waves that made the fluid from the shots come out in long beads rather than as a continuous stream, so that the recipients were being hit with tiny "BBs" as opposed to a gentle fluid. This type of problem, requiring knowledge of physical laws or biological principles, fascinates Joan. "Once we understand the physics or bioprocesses of what we are interested in, the answers to the problems are almost obvious."

Joan developed her interest in prosthetics when she saw that the issue of the discomfort for patients was an issue of mechanical force between the limbs and the sockets. She thought she could help solve the problem by understanding interface mechanics—the study of how the limb meets the prosthesis. Joan sold her ideas to some university departments, who helped fund her research, and got some more money from grants so she could do research for her Ph.D. "Wherever I could find money to support my small salary as a graduate assistant and the equipment expenses, I'd do it. I consulted with companies, which is lucrative if you do it right. During the last year and one half of my Ph.D. work, an independent research foundation in prosthetics hired me as an employee. I directed their bioengineering program for awhile."

In her leisure time, Joan likes to play volleyball, bike ride, windsurf, ride horses, and more recently, play basketball. Having just bought her own home, Joan spends much time remodeling and keeping up the house and land, an effort for which her engineering background often comes in handy.

# Daniela Santeju

Daniela Santeju

**Dimensional Control Systems and Variational Systems Analysis**

**Engineer,** Tower Automotive Technical Center, Farmington Hills, MI

Major in Engineering; master's degree in Mechanical Engineering

# Mechanical
# Engineer,
# Automotive

## CAD/CAM Wizard

Daniela Santeiu teaches engineers how to use CAD/CAM (three-dimensional computer aided design, computer aided manufacture) software. She works for Tower Automotive, a medium-sized company that designs parts for cars—things like hinges, frames, pillars, control arms, and other structural components.

Daniela is the first engineer at her company who learned the new software. A major car manufacturer that buys the parts her company designs wanted Tower Automotive to begin designing with SDRC (software made by Structural Dynamic Research Corporation). Now that she is an expert, she can teach other engineers at Tower and give them SDRC certification.

# DANIELA'S CAREER PATH

Meets distant relatives
▼ from U.S., starts
corresponding

Gets interested
▼ in mechanical
engineering

Studies
▼ engineering

SDRC has been on the market for only a few years. Engineers use it to design in a three-dimensional way called solid modeling. That way, an engineer can see a part from every angle and how it will fit with other parts of the car, and with the car's frame. Next, a drawing is made of the bility. Then, the part is manufactured. Before this software was available, the parts were designed using a two-dimensional software that was not as easy to use in evaluating and manufacturing the part. It was harder to design the part so that it would work with the rest of the parts in the car.

[ This is a very good career. It's not noisy or dirty. There is always a lot happening and you can continue to learn. ]

part and the part design is analyzed to see whether the part can withhold all of the stresses that it will have—like the pressure from the weight of other parts pressing against it, or the heat of the engine. The design for the part is modified as needed to meet requirements for stress, load, and dura-

Daniela certifies the engineers who have demonstrated that they know how to use the new CAD/CAM software and can pass the required tests. In the future, design engineers will need this certification to get a job at a place like her company, she says. In her classroom at the company, she

Visits U.S., likes
▼ car factory

Gets master's in
▼ mechanical engineering

Gets job at Tower
▼ doing testing

teaches three engineers at a time, each on their own computer. Daniela also helps them on the job when they need it.

To learn to teach the SDRC software, Daniela had to attend class for three months. In the first month, she learned simple modeling techniques. In the second month, she became a teacher's assistant. In the third month, she actually taught the SDRC class.

Daniela would go home at night and practice teaching on her husband, Vanja, who also is an engineer (he designs tools). "The more people asked me questions, the better I got," she says. "At first it was hard to teach because I speak English with an accent. But I taught English in my country before I came to the United States, so that helped."

# Home in
## Industrial Brasov

Daniela grew up in Brasov, Romania, one of the most industrial cities in that Eastern European country. She remembers, as a girl, that Brasov was filled with truck and tractor factories. Daniela, who liked to take things apart from a very young age, wanted to be a mechanical engineer and work in one of the factories. Her grades were good enough to get a scholarship to the University of Transylvania in Brasov to study mechanical engineering. "In Romania, if you did well in school, you could get your education paid for up through your master's degree. It's not like here where you have to pay the schools. They actually give you money to study."

Being an engineering student was hard. Most of the other students were

51

# DANIELA'S CAREER PATH

**Moves to** finite
element analysis

**Teaches** CAD/CAM
software

males, and many of them could practice tinkering with the family car. But there was no way that Daniela's dad was going to let her touch his car! There were 100 men and only 5 women in her class at the university, and the young women felt they had to study harder and read more, to be as well-regarded as the men.

In 1989, when communism started to fail in Eastern Europe, it wasn't a stable time for Romania, which was a communist country. Daniela finished her undergraduate degree and visited distant relatives in the United States, people she'd had met one day, when she was 11, at her grandfather's house in Romania. They visited and were looking for their Romanian ancestors. Daniela was the only one in the family who spoke any English. She got to know these visitors and began writing

to them. "It was annoying when they sent back my letters corrected in red pen to the proper English, but in the long run that turned out to be very good for me."

Daniela got to see inside a Ford factory during this 1989 visit. She decided she would like to work in a car factory as an engineer. She went home to study some more to give herself a better chance of getting this type of job. She got her master's degree in mechanical engineering, graduating 12th in her class. But she couldn't get a job in engineering in Romania because there weren't any jobs—most of the factories had closed. Instead, she taught English to high school students as a substitute teacher for two years and dreamed about coming to the United States again.

In 1994, she visited the Detroit,

Michigan, area again. She got a job with Tower Automotive at the end of November on the strength of her engineering degree. She had applied to Tower because it was only 6 miles from where she was living and she thought she could either get a ride with someone or ride her bike to work, since she did not drive at the time. "I felt very proud that for the first time in my life, someone (Tower) was willing to give me a job based on my education."

## A Creative First Job

Tower management wanted Daniela to do tests on the car parts that Tower designed and manufactured before they were sent to customers. They wanted to be sure parts would work right and not fail. They gave Daniela an empty room and some college students—interns getting work experience—as helpers. She gradually filled the room with car frames (from Tower's customers: Ford, Chrysler, and General Motors), that she had begged from their engineers. She and

## CAREER CHECKLIST ✔

### You'll like this job if you ...

Are good at analysis and logical problem solving

Like to work independently

Like to learn new things

Are realistic about how to get things done

Are good with mechanical things and spatial relationships

Can explain things so others will pay attention and understand them

the interns began testing the parts on these car frames to see whether the parts were strong enough.

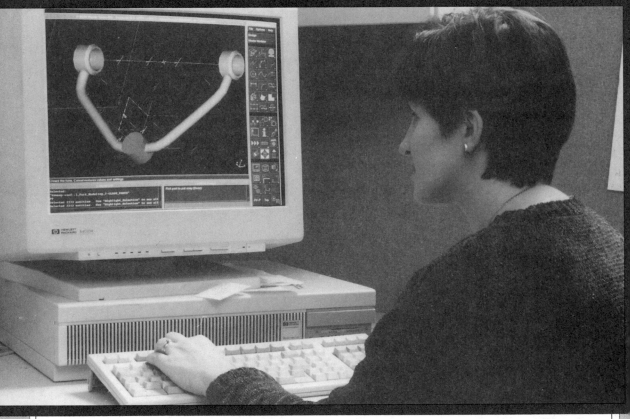

For example, they had to test whether a hinge that closed a car trunk could go through 40,000 cycles (go up and down 40,000 times), which was the required standard for that part. In order to make sure the part was able to meet the standard, they had to simu-late everything the way it would really happen—weight, height, angle of opening. Daniela and the interns also tested what would happen to some of these parts in a car crash. They tested metal to see at what temperature it weakened and became deformed, which would put the part in danger of not holding.

"This was a very good first job for an engineer. I was my own boss and allowed to be creative in how we did the tests. We had a lot of fun designing those tests, and I learned a lot about how parts worked with other parts and what to look for when you were analyzing them."

computer could simulate conditions for loads, buckling, and durability. The computer showed red "hot spots" where the element of the part would fail. If these red spots weren't in the places they were expected to be, something was wrong with the part design. A part had to be divided into lots of small elements, sometimes a thousand of them fitting together, like in a

# [ When I was learning the CAD/CAM software, it was really exciting. At the end of the day, I had designed a car component. ]

Daniela thinks Tower took a risk in hiring her. Her English wasn't very good, so it was hard to tell what she really knew. After she had worked in testing for awhile, the company realized how smart she was, and they moved her to the finite element analysis group. There, she worked on a computer to simulate the conditions that a part would experience. The

puzzle. It would take a human being days to do this, but the computer could do it in half an hour, using values collected from engineers who worked on the cars.

"In my company, about 35 percent of the engineers are now women. Women like working in finite element analysis because the job requires strong analytical and organizational

# JOB FACTS

**HOURS:** 8:30 to 5:00

**WORKPLACE:** Large classroom with six computer workstations; office cubicle
Test rooms and manufacturing floor, also visits various locations where individual engineers work

**CLOTHES:** Business clothes, overalls, safety gear (shoes, hard hat, goggles).

**DUTIES:** Teach computer design software to designers and engineers. Design new products. Do analysis of product as it moves through the manufacturing process.

**$ALARY:** Mechanical Engineer
Starting salary $37,338 to $53,933

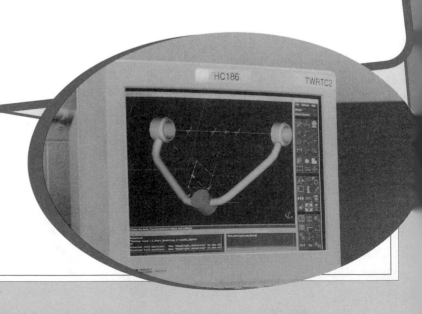

skills and less interaction with the customer, who is the engineer at the car company. Sometimes these engineers can be pretty intimidating. They have been at the car company a long time, and they like to argue. Engineers like to argue about how to do things the best way anyway, but when they are arguing with a woman they can be even more insistent. With this job, you are pretty much on your own. You are given the job and the due date, and how you achieve that objective is up to you. Most of the time you determine your own hours."

# Keeps on Learning

Daniela loves the fact that she keeps learning at Tower. First she learned to do tests on car parts, then she learned to use the computer to do finite element analysis, and then she learned to do dimensional control analysis. "No part is perfect. All parts are slightly imperfect. It's good to have a little tolerance in the part, so that the part can fit the frame of the car and you can lower the cost of the part. You put the values in the computer and see how to adjust the part so it has the right tolerance."

Daniela's husband, Vanja, was one of the interns who worked in testing. The couple has been married about a year and one half and has just had a daughter, Emma. Daniela's mother came to take care of Emma for six months and to meet her new son-in-law! Daniela, who took three months' leave, went back to work. She's planning to work from home one day a week, on the day when she will be doing mostly inputting into the computer.

# Monica Brooks

Monica Brooks

**Senior Engineer,** Precision Mechanical Design Group, Lockheed Martin, Orlando, FL

Major in Mechanical Engineering, master's degree in Mechanical Engineering

# Mechanical Engineer, Aerospace

## She Helps Pilots See in the Dark

**B**orn and raised in Indianapolis, Indiana, Monica Brooks surprised everyone when, after graduating from college, she moved away from family and friends to accept a job with a large corporation in Orlando, Florida.

"I knew I would move for a good job," says Monica. "And that first year, everyone sure enjoyed coming down to visit me here in Central Florida."

Today, 15 years later, Monica still enjoys her job as a part of the Precision Mechanical Design Department at Lockheed Martin, a company that does work for the U.S. Department of Defense on several contracts. "I like working for a large company," she says. "You have a chance to do a lot of

# MONICA'S CAREER PATH

Plays sports with
▼ brother

Learns from
▼ Dad how to
   fix things

Enjoys math and
▼ science

different things. And there are a lot of different types of engineers working here. In the design area, the company projects come in to be designed, then

copters. The equipment will be installed on helicopters to improve how pilots see at night. (Perhaps you have seen infrared images of this night vi-

> **Don't underestimate yourself. You can do whatever you like. Ask people lots of questions about what they do and listen carefully to what they say.**

move to the production area for the next phase, and we engineers get a new project to design."

Monica's first job with the company, formerly called Martin Marietta, was as an associate engineer. Her first project was working on improving the design of a missile. She advanced to engineer and is now senior engineer. Her current project, a long-term one, is a program to provide infrared optical equipment for military heli-

sion on television or in the movies.)

"When we get a job to design, we are given requirements—like the equipment must be a certain size, but not weigh over a certain weight, and must be made of a certain material. I like the design phase at the beginning, laying it out. You try your ideas—if it is too heavy you might decide to cut holes in the material to make it lighter. I really enjoy getting my own project, working on it, then bringing it back. I like the technical part, the design part."

Monica has a desk and her own computer in a cubicle she shares with another engineer. She also works in a large room where there are eight large-screen computers. Each engineer is working on a piece of the whole, so it helps them to work side by side and be able to ask each other questions. All the pieces must fit together and meet the requirements.

After deciding on a design, Monica makes the drawings. When the drawings are finished, the parts are built and tested to see if they fit together and work, meeting the stated requirements. "Test engineers do the testing, but we often have to go to the testing labs to explain how we designed it, why we did it the way we did, and to help them when they are assembling it.

Sometimes they will tell us we have to change it. For example, we might have to mount it a different way to get the results we want. So we alter our parts."

When everything tests out okay, a prototype is built and delivered to the customer. If the customer is satisfied, then the equipment goes into production and many copies are delivered to the customer. "We have what we call 'win' parties, after the prototypes are delivered and accepted and the company gets the new contract."

# A Summertime Discovery

Monica was a tomboy growing up on a block with few boys. Her older brother, Gregory, taught her football, basketball, and baseball so he'd have someone to play with. Her father liked to fix things around the house

# MONICA'S CAREER PATH

Buys car,
then condo

Gets master's degree

and work on cars. When Monica showed an interest or asked questions, he'd always tell her how to do things—like change the car's oil or work on the brakes or wire a lamp. Both her father, a policeman, and her mother, who worked at a finance cen-

ter, always told her she could do anything she wanted to do.

Monica didn't learn about engineering until she was in high school in In-

dianapolis. She enjoyed math and science and was on the tennis team and in math club. She thought maybe she'd become a doctor, because she liked helping people. Then she decided to check out a new minority engineering program. She attended the Minority Engineering Advancement Program (MEAP) summer sessions after her freshman, sophomore, and junior years. It was given by the Indianapolis branch of Purdue University. "I enjoyed it. Each week we learned about a different type of engineering. For electrical engineering we made our own radio, for computer engineering we created a program to draw a circle, for industrial engineering we poured molten metal and made a nameplate, and for mechanical engineering we built a mousetrap car—the snap of the trap made the car go—and raced them to see whose car could go the farthest."

When she graduated from high school, Monica applied for and got a scholarship through MEAP. She chose biomedical engineering, thinking still of her interest in medicine. "Then I saw that with a degree in mechanical engineering you could do so many types of work. I could still do biomedical if I wanted to. I thought if I got a job that I didn't like, having the mechanical engineering degree would make it easier to switch to another type of job."

Once Monica started college, she and her friends in engineering spent most of their time studying. "I tutored math a little, but didn't have to work because of my scholarship and because I lived at home." While there were some women students in engineering program, there were fewer in the mechanical engineering specialty. "By the time I finished, the last few classes were mostly guys, and of the 100 graduates in ME, only 4 or 5 were

## CAREER CHECKLIST ✔

# You'll like this job if you ...

Can analyze things and solve problems

Can think up new ways to do things

Will study hard

Are precise and accurate in your work

Enjoy learning new things

Like to work indoors

# JOB FACTS

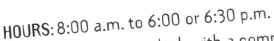

**HOURS:** 8:00 a.m. to 6:00 or 6:30 p.m.

**OFFICE:** Has her own desk with a computer in a cubicle she shares with another engineer. Often works on big-screen computers in a large room along side other engineers.

**CLOTHES:** Casual business clothes.

**DUTIES:** Designs new, small parts of equipment, which have to fit with other parts being designed by coworkers, according to specific requirements. Prepares drawings.

**$ALARY:** Mechanical Engineer

Starting $40,000

Associate $40,000 to $50,000

Senior $50,000 to $60,000

women." Monica was the first Purdue graduate of the minority engineering program at the campus of Indiana University-Purdue University at Indianapolis.

Just before graduation, Monica listed her name and resume in a publication that went out to interested companies. She got a call to come for an interview in Florida and accepted the job they offered.

# Long Hours and Cross Stitch

While Monica's regular hours are 8 to 5, she often has to work overtime. There are deadlines to meet, so the engineers have to keep working to get the work done on time. When Monica decided to get her master's degree (the company would pay her tuition), she took one course at a time, because she knew she would be putting in extra hours at work. She also had to take in-plant training whenever the company had new software or equip-

ment that the engineers had to learn. "When I look back, I don't know how I did all that work and studying, plus playing softball on the company's coed league, all at one time. It took me four-and-one-half years, but it was worth it. Now that I have my degree along with my work experience, I feel more confident and secure about getting another job, should the company downsize and lay off a lot of us engineers."

When Monica first started her job, she and another new hire were the only women mechanical engineers on her project. "Management put us together, so we worked together on the project. It was nice to have another woman to talk to. Now there are several women, and we stick together. We

have an informal group that meets once a month after work hours in someone's home. The guys tease us about our 'sewing bee.' We do cross stitch, eat a dessert, and talk about what happened at work. It's our support group. We can help new women engineers learn how the company operates, where to go to get things done, and what to watch out for."

Monica lives just 15 minutes away from work, so she has an easy commute unless she has to go to the Lockheed plant across town. When she first came to town she rented a furnished apartment. "The first year I saved money and bought my own furniture. The second year I bought a car. The third year, I bought my condo."

Now that she has completed her master's degree, Monica has more time for fun things like bike riding, working out at the gym, going to movies, and ice skating. "When it's hot here in Florida, we enjoy cooling off at the ice-skating rink." Monica also volunteers and recently helped judge an event at an engineering fair for students. "The students had to build a container for an egg and then drop it without breaking the egg. They had the mousetrap car and a solar car race too."

## Family Reunions

Monica likes to travel, so vacations are usually spent visiting interesting places with friends or family. Several stone Park, Grand Canyon, lots of interesting places." When Monica visited a friend in Colorado, she went bungee jumping. "My friends would not do it, so they took my picture. It was fun."

Once a year, she goes to a family reunion. "My father has 9 brothers and sisters. We all meet in a different city in the summertime. Every other year I go to visit my mother's family in Washington, DC." Monica is enjoying the single lifestyle, but may be getting

> If you like math, science, and mechanical things, don't be ashamed when kids call you a nerd. You will be able to do a lot with those skills. Two plus two is always going to be four and you can use that knowledge.

times Monica, her nephew, her mother, and her aunt have planned a trip to a "new place" they've never seen. "We've been to Alaska, Yellow- pressure from the family. She says, "If I meet the right person, that would be okay too."

# Tracey Smith

**Senior Engineer,** Orbital Transportation Management Systems Division, Orbital Sciences Corp., Gaithersburg, MD

Major in Electrical Engineering, master's degree in Electrical Engineering, Communications

# Electrical Engineer

## A Sound Analysis

Tracey Smith loves her job because every day she gets to do something new. In fact, she gets to do a lot of different things. Some tasks are repetitive, but there always seems to be a new problem to solve, something new to learn, and interesting people to work with.

Tracey is a senior engineer at Orbital Sciences Corporation in the Orbital Transportation Management Systems Division, or as they call it, the TMS division. Her office is in Gaithersburg, Maryland. The company sells products that track vehicles. Their primary system is the ORBTRAC-300, which is used by bus companies. "The system lets dispatchers see where the buses are at all times," says Tracey. "Dispatchers can, with the push of a button, communicate with the drivers about schedules or traffic or any other important information. The bus drivers can also talk with the dispatcher. In an emergency,

the driver can secretly push a silent alarm button to alert the dispatcher. The console in the bus automatically switches to a microphone so that the dispatcher can hear and eavesdrop on what is going on in the bus, such as a sick driver, an accident, or a robbery. This safety feature helps the driver get help, even if she can't ask for it." Similar systems are also used to communicate with trains, snowplows, and other fleets of vehicles.

Tracey is involved in developing these systems for different clients. "The system ORBTRAC-300 gives the dispatchers two screens. One shows a map with a different symbol for each bus, and the other shows messages to and from the buses," says Tracey. "I work on developing different parts of the system. I draft drawings of equipment, write documentation, set-up and test equipment, research new products, and write proposals. I also travel to

New York to meet with contractors and examine equipment."

"Potential customers will send RFPs (requests for proposals), which basically say 'this is what the we are looking for.' We prepare a proposal—'this is what we can provide you.' Sometimes, different engineers write certain sections of the proposal. I have written the communications section a couple of times."

To write her part of the proposal, Tracey must gather information about how and where the client's com-

pany operates its buses. She works with contractors to select the best sites for antennas that will transmit the radio frequencies—from the building where dispatchers are, to the antenna site, to the moving vehicles, and back again from driver to antenna to dispatcher. If she finds problems such as coverage concerns (the radio frequencies won't reach important areas), she figures out how to solve them. She puts it all together and writes it up as her part of the proposal.

# TRACEY'S CAREER PATH

Gets master's degree

Joins Orbital, communications engineering

## Confidence Building at College

Tracey is comfortable meeting new people or standing up before a group to explain an engineering project she has worked on. She wasn't always comfortable, though. Growing up in Olney, Maryland, Tracey was a shy girl. She and her twin sister Stacey had lots of friends, but Tracey was shy about meeting new people. At school she liked science and took all the math courses through calculus. By her senior year in high school, she began to serve on school committees (like the homecoming committee) and had a boyfriend. "That took up a lot of my time."

Tracey didn't discover engineering until she was 17 and had to decide what she would study in college. "The only engineer I knew about was the one who drives a train," she says. "Since I loved math and science, engineering appealed to me because you get to do a lot of problem solving using both math and science. However, I still wasn't sure what engineers did. I chose electrical engineering because it was the toughest to get into. I figured if I didn't like it, it would be easier to transfer to another type of engineering."

Both Tracey and Stacey chose electrical engineering at the University of Maryland in College Park. In the large freshman classes, there were about 25 women and 125 men. "My parents raised us free of stereotypes. There were no girl toys or boy toys. We were encouraged to try anything that interested us. I had a Barbie doll, action figures, racecar sets, and microscopes. They never taught me that there were limits."

Tracey loved electrical engineering. "You definitely had to do a lot of studying, but there was time to have fun." She made a decision that she would try lots of new things and get involved in different activities. One of these was to play sports—racquetball, archery, working out with weights. "I think exercise is so important, mentally and physically."

Tracey also joined a sorority and groups for engineering students, taking leadership roles. She made the National Dean's List and won the Outstanding Senior Award from the University of Maryland's chapter of the National Electrical Engineering Honor Society. "The more you do, even though it scares you, the more comfortable you are doing it. The more I took on responsibilities, the easier it got. My confidence went up. It was very rewarding."

During her junior year, Tracey enrolled in the cooperative education program. It meant it would take five years to get her degree, but it pro-

## CAREER CHECKLIST ✓

### You'll like this job if you ...

Like to be exposed to a steady stream of new information

Can communicate well

Like to make things work efficiently

Like math and science

Are curious about the world around you

Like to ask a lot of questions

Like to learn

Want to know how things work

Enjoy reading

Like to travel

Can set priorities and organize your time

# JOB FACTS

**HOURS:** 8:00 to 5:00

**WORKPLACE:** An office with a door, which she shares with another person. Has her own desk, file cabinet, bookshelf, and computer.

**CLOTHES:** Business clothes on Monday through Thursdays. Casual clothes on Fridays and for travel. (Even jeans!)

**DUTIES:** Analyzes customer's project requirements. Develops proposals that show how the company can provide an efficient communication system. Works with contractors to establish antenna sites. Drafts drawings of equipment. Writes documentation. Sets up and tests equipment. Researches new products. Writes proposals. Travels.

**$ALARY:** Electrical and Electronics Engineer
        Starting $37,300
        10 years' experience $61,000 median

vided work experience. It was also a big confidence builder. "I highly recommend cooperative education in any field. You learn what you will be doing when you get out of college. It gives you a good feel for what you want to do, where you want to do it, and what kind of employers you want to look for."

## Sonar and Submarines

Tracey's co-op employer was the Department of Defense David Taylor Research Center in Bethesda, Maryland. There, Tracey learned how to work

through water. The submarine is equipped with transducers. When the sound waves hit the transducers, they cause pressure (SPLs—sound pressure levels). The pressure is converted by the transducer into electricity, which is then processed by the equipment."

In Tracey's department, the engineers designed the sonar equipment

**The things you do in school, including getting good grades, count on your resume and help you get interviews.**

with sonar. "Sonar is the equipment that allows the submarine to see and hear underwater. Sound waves travel

and wrote plans on how to test it. Then, they went on board submarines to conduct the testing. They supervised the sailors who were doing testing and wrote up the test results. Tracey had to get a special "clearance" from the government to work on this

military equipment. "I couldn't tell my roommates exactly what I was doing."

Tracey was the only female engineer where she worked. "It was military and a male-dominated environment. Only men were stationed on the subs. I would run into some people who were not accustomed to working with female engineers. Sometimes, I'd get the feeling they were uncomfortable working with me."

Tracey also got to travel—to Seattle, Washington; Norfolk, Virginia; San Diego, California; and Groton, Connecticut—to attend meetings and supervise testing.

After her year of co-op ended, Tracey had one more year of college. As her December graduation approached, she decided she would stay on and get a master's degree. She received a teaching assistant (TA) position to help pay expenses. "I really enjoyed helping the undergraduate students. It was my most rewarding time in graduate school. I loved taking the things that had been hard for me and making them easier to understand. It was so rewarding when the students 'got it.' "

After completing one year at graduate school, Tracey decided to go back to work. David Taylor

Research Center welcomed her back. She was given more responsibilities and her own projects to manage. She traveled even more. One of the places she traveled to was Hawaii. "We were working on equipment for submarines docked in Pearl Harbor." The government would fly Tracey to Hawaii, where she would get a rental car and hotel room. She would also get a "per diem," an amount of money to spend

each day on food and other necessary expenses.

"We worked whatever shift was appropriate to test the equipment—4 p.m. to midnight, 11 p.m. to 6 a.m., or the day shift. It depended on when the ship was available. I would supervise and help conduct the testing, and then write up the results." When she wasn't working Tracey had time to lie on the beach and drive around the island.

Besides the travel, there were lots of meetings to attend. Tracey had to give presentations to the department's sponsor, the Office of Naval Intelligence, so that the department could continue to receive its funding.

Tracey learned to give these presentations step by step. "First, a more experienced engineer would have me give a small part of the presentation, but he would answer any questions that were asked. By the time I was giving the complete presentation, I had learned what to expect, how to think before speaking, and had honed my skills in answering on-the-spot questions."

In three years, Tracey had saved enough money to return to graduate school and finish her degree. "I wanted to move from underwater acoustics to communications engineering. Underwater acoustics engineering deals with the properties of underwater sound and the design of equipment that measures it. Communications engineering deals with getting information from one place to another through the air or through wire. Some examples include radios, cellular phones, televisions, and satellites. Communications is a fast growing field that has many new and exciting challenges."

With her master's degree in electrical engineering, communications, Tracey went job hunting. Within four months, she took a job with Orbital Sciences.

## Skiing and Scuba Diving

Tracey believes in keeping active during her leisure hours. She enjoys bik-

> The more often you try new activities and take on leadership roles, even though they scare you, the easier it gets. It gives you confidence.

ing, racquetball, and working out. Her boyfriend is on the ski patrol at a nearby ski area, so she does a lot of dies. There, she did 10 or more dives and earned an advanced scuba diving certification. Maybe she will use her

# Communications engineering deals with getting information from one place to another through the air or through wire.

skiing. Her latest interest is scuba diving. She took classes in a swimming pool in town, but to get her certification she traveled with friends to the Cayman Islands in the West In-

engineering know-how and develop some personal sonar gear so she can locate the type of fish she wants to see or a shipwreck she wants to explore.

# JoAnne Walser

JoAnne Walser

**Major, Engineer,** United States Army; **Instructor**, Department of Geography and Environmental Engineering, United States Military Academy at West Point, NY

Major in Chemical Engineering, master's degree in Environmental Engineering

# Engineer, U.S. Army Corps of Engineers

## Major Challenges in the Corps

The United States Army paid for JoAnne Walser's undergraduate college education—a degree in chemical engineering from Penn State University. The Army even sent her to graduate school at the University of Florida for a master's degree in environmental engineering. JoAnne has had a fascinating and challenging career using engineering, leadership, and management skills in the United States, Germany, and Bosnia as an Army lieutenant, captain, and now as a major.

Today, JoAnne is the highest ranking woman in the Army who has served as a combat engineer. (She was the first woman to command combat engineers in a division.) She commanded Army platoons and compa- nies, had responsibility for the main- tenance of large equipment (trucks, boats, and bulldozers), served as a general's aide, and has managed pro- jects that cost as much as $270 mil- lion. She made sure 25,000 soldiers had places to sleep and eat in Bosnia when the United States sent a peace- keeping mission to that country. JoAnne's current assignment is to teach environmental engineering and physical geography at West Point, the Army's top school for officers. But soon she will move on to another school as a student, once again. She will learn the leadership skills that she will need to command a battalion of soldiers.

## Duties and Challenges

JoAnne's career illustrates what a woman can do in today's Army. Each step has led her to more management and leadership responsibility, more challenges, and more visibility among high-ranking Army officers. She gets to use her engineering knowledge in solving difficult problems for the Army, although, she says, it's the people skills and not the technical skills that are most important to her success.

JoAnne says one of the most inter- esting things she has done to date was to figure out how to house soldiers moving into Bosnia in late 1995. She was in Germany at the time, working as the brigade logistics officer for the headquarters company in Engineer Brigade, 1st Armored Division. This company supported soldiers in com-

Commands platoon,
designs Panama pier

Goes to Germany,
commands a company

Serves as general's
aide, commands
another company

bat. JoAnne helped plan the logistics (movement of troops, supplies, and equipment) for the entire brigade. As the brigade logistics officer, she also worked for the assistant division commander for support, a general, and she was "his engineer." That meant

with an answer," he said. JoAnne was alarmed at having to work so fast, but she was lucky. In one of her previous Army jobs, she had worked as the assistant executive officer to the deputy chief of staff of engineers for the U.S. Army of Europe. This position re-

> If you want to be an engineer with only four years in school, you'll really have to work at it. It's not easy and even brilliant people have to work very hard. It's not a course of study you take if you are interested in playing while you are in school.

that whatever engineering question her boss asked, she had to answer.

It all started one morning when the general came to her and asked her how they were going to house the soldiers. "You have 24 hours to come up

quired that she be the aide to a one-star general, who was responsible for the military aspects of engineering and all the Army construction going on in Europe as well as environmental issues. In this job, she had traveled

# JoANNE'S CAREER PATH

Becomes brigade
▼ logistics officer, houses
soldiers in Bosnia

Gets master's degree,
▼ teaches at West Point

all over Germany and Eastern Europe. She got to know many of the Army engineering officers as well as the contractors who worked with them. She knew that a certain U.S. engineering firm would build whatever was requested on short notice.

So she spent the day calling people she knew who had some of the answers she needed—what was the best housing for soldiers in Bosnia, what sorts of kitchens and toilets would work best, what was the most economical material, what was the most durable material? She also found out how bitter the Bosnian winters were, so that she would know the best type of housing to recommend for various areas in that country. At the end of her prescribed 24-hour period, she was able to put together a plan.

## Bosnia Base Camps

JoAnne recommended that the Army buy sleeping "containers" for the soldiers as well as other containers for the kitchen, showers, and toilets for parts of Bosnia where the snow fell heavily and the winter was fierce. "For other parts of the country, where the winter was milder, Army tents would be more suitable," she said. The containers to be built by the engineering firm are similar to house trailers, only smaller. They can be moved by tractor trailer and plugged into each other and then into a power source, so electricity and heat reach them.

It very quickly became apparent that JoAnne couldn't perform both her regular duties as logistics officer, where her responsibilities consisted of arranging the transportation for the supplies and equipment for her own brigade (which had grown from 1,000 to 5,400 people during this time), and this larger project, which required that she supervise the container construction and the building of 25 base camps. After the initial deployment to Bosnia, the Army brought in a major to take over JoAnne's logistic officer job (she was a captain at that point). For seven months, until she left to attend graduate school back in the United States, JoAnne was in charge of managing this project. When First Lady Hillary Rodham Clinton came to Bosnia, JoAnne briefed her on how soldiers were housed.

"The time I spent in Bosnia was personally and professionally incredible," JoAnne says. "Instead of just working with engineers, I established a reputation with the maneuver folks—infantry, armor, and all the brigade commanders. Every time the U.S. Army Europe Commander, a four-star general, came into the country, I ended up escorting him around. Here I was, a captain, and most of the people I was interacting with were lieutenant

## CAREER CHECKLIST

### You'll like this job if you ...

Are tenacious

Will take charge when in charge and will follow orders when appropriate

Can prove yourself over and over again in new situations

Can get along with all types of people

Won't mind moving, maybe once a year

Like to manage big projects

Always want to improve your skills

Are able to keep both long-term and short-term goals in mind

# JOB FACTS

**HOURS:** 0730 to 1730 (7:30 a.m. to 5:30 p.m.)

**WORKPLACE:** West Point classroom

**CLOTHES:** Uniform

**DUTIES:** Uses mapping experience and environmental studies knowledge to instruct cadets

**SALARY:** Salaries vary with rank and time in the service. A lieutenant makes approximately $30,000; major approximately $50,000.

colonel and above; but everybody knew the one-star general (her boss) was behind me and supported me."

# It Started with College ROTC

JoAnne's career with the Army actually began with ROTC in college. In love with horses, and having arranged to get herself a horse at the age of 12, JoAnne dreamed all through high school of being a veterinarian. In junior high school JoAnne had taken lots of math and science courses. In fact, by the time she had finished ninth grade in Broomall, Pennsylvania, she also had taken courses in chemistry, biology, and physics.

In high school, she continued her love of math and science, taking two years each of chemistry, physics, and biology as well as some calculus. About this time, her parents, who had once said they would help her go to college, could no longer afford to do so. One of her friend's brothers, whom she admired, recommended that she

talk to the Navy about getting a college scholarship. The Navy recruiter asked her what she might be interested in studying, and JoAnne said she thought the nuclear engineering program sounded interesting. "You

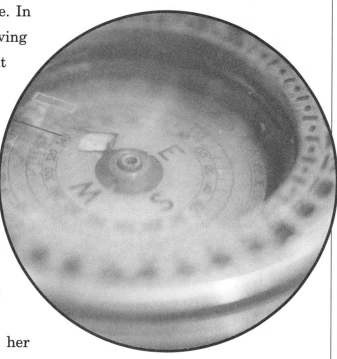

can't do that," the man said. "We don't allow women in that program."

So JoAnne talked to an Army recruiter and said she wanted to study veterinary medicine or engineering. "Well," he said, "it's difficult to get the Army to send you to school to be a vet-

## How the Army is Organized

### Army Commissioned Officers

general (four star)

lieutenant general (three star)

major general (two star)

brigadier general (one star)

colonel

lieutenant colonel

major

captain

first lieutenant

second lieutenant

### Army Groups (from largest down)

Corps

Division

Brigade

Battalion

Company

Platoon

that boarded 26 horses. The woman who owned the farm gave her room and board and a little spending money in exchange for JoAnne taking care of the horses. JoAnne would get up in the morning, feed the horses, then let them out into the pasture, clean the stalls, and then go to class. In the afternoon, she would put the horses back in the stalls, feed them, and then study until about 11:00 at night. She was very motivated to keep her grades up so that she could get her scholarship.

At the end of her first year of college, she demonstrated her leadership abilities. She was the first woman put in charge of her ROTC detachment, with responsibility for making sure people went where they were supposed to, and taking charge during formations. She also was named the superior cadet for her detachment for that year.

erinarian, but if you want to study engineering and you can keep your grades above a 3.0 the first year, I can just about guarantee that you can get a three-year scholarship."

JoAnne attended Penn State, majoring in chemical engineering. She found a place to live near the campus by offering to clean the stalls at a farm

## Learning to be a Leader

The Army gave JoAnne her scholarship, and she promised to spend four years in active duty or eight years in the Army Reserves after she graduated from college. The summer after her junior year of college, the Army sent her to a six-week summer camp, where she was evaluated against her peers. Her performance at summer camp was one of the key considerations used to determine whether she would get selected to go into the reserve or to active duty. She got selected for active duty. After this camp, JoAnne was sent to Fort Belvoir, Virginia, for three weeks. During this cadet leadership training, she took over the command of a platoon for a platoon leader who went on leave, an exercise all the cadets in leadership training had to complete. She had to deal with the problems of the platoon, including trying to find a soldier who had gone AWOL (absent without leave) because of personal problems and coping with the stress that the soldier's action caused the 25-member platoon, which was mostly male.

In May of 1986, JoAnne was commissioned as an officer. She married, but her husband was in the Navy and had to leave for training while she stayed at Penn State where she worked as an ROTC recruiter. She enjoyed talking to women about what ROTC was like, dispelling their fears and stressing that it wasn't as physically demanding as they might have imagined. JoAnne is only 5 feet 2 inches tall, and, she says, she is not capable of great physical strength.

JoAnne's first assignment was working with the Army Corps of Engineers (one of 17 women chosen that year) at a construction company at Fort Eustis, Virginia. There she learned about the company, figured out exactly what they did, and was made a platoon leader. She had 24 soldiers under her supervision and was responsible for transportation and maintenance of big equipment—including boats, 10-ton tractor-trailer trucks, bulldozers, and a Delong pier (equipment that is used to create a pier in the water so that big boats can load onto smaller ones that can reach the shore). One time, her superior officer was called and asked how long it would take to unload an oil tanker. JoAnne was the only one in her unit who could figure that out, because her superior officer and his assistant weren't engineers. All she had to do was to use an engineering equation on fluid flow called Bernoulli's equation.

JoAnne had to give up her platoon when she was four months pregnant. She worked in the supply room until it was time to take maternity leave. When she returned to work after her daughter, Elizabeth, was born, she was made an engineer staff officer at

site and design the piers. She was only in Panama 10 days, but she spent two months back home ordering the right materials such as pilings (telephone poles), which were not available inside Panama. She also had to arrange for shipping these materials into Panama.

About this time, JoAnne and her husband decided to divorce. It was difficult to be a married couple, JoAnne says, since she and her husband each

> To continue to succeed in the Army, you need to be an executive officer or an operations officer at the battalion level. You need to be selective in the jobs you choose, so that you will have the right experience to move up.

the battalion level. Her job was to find construction projects for the construction unit at Fort Eustis. She uncovered the need for pier renovation in Panama by speaking with other engineers in the Army. They wanted to upgrade the Panama pier so that bigger ships could anchor there. JoAnne traveled to Panama to evaluate the

had separate careers in the service and went to separate schools and had separate lives. "When I counsel young cadets, I advise them not to marry until they have been in the Army for a year or so. This gives them time to 'find' themselves and establish their career before committing themselves to another person."

## A Decision to Stay

JoAnne finished her tour at Fort Eustis just as her required four years in the Army were up. She thought about trying to find a job in the private sector, but first asked the Army if they would send her to Germany as a captain in a topographic (map making) unit. The Army gave her what she wanted.

In April of 1991, she and daughter Elizabeth headed for Heidelberg, Germany. Her first year there, she served as the adjutant (personnel officer) for a battalion of 460 people. The second year, she commanded a company. "The Army tries to give captains the opportunity to command a company at some point in their career." She was responsible for 150 soldiers and millions of dollars of equipment. Her soldiers, topographic experts, were located in five different areas in Germany, and she traveled to the different areas to make sure they had what they needed. During the weekends, she and her daughter would often visit other nearby countries.

Her commanding officer, a colonel, was a woman. "The whole time I was at Fort Eustis, I was the only woman engineer officer, but now I had women officers to talk to. I've always tried to be one of the guys, and that's why I've done well in the Army, but it was still great to have women officers to talk to."

## Fascinated with the Ocean

When JoAnne began deep-sea scuba diving, she decided she wanted to study environmental engineering. She was fascinated with the sea and waterways and wanted to see how she could contribute to preserving the beauty of the ocean. She was able to get a scholarship from West Point to go to graduate school. She had to promise to teach at West Point for three years after she finished getting her master's degree.

# Lisa Litz-Montanaro

Lisa Litz-Montanaro

**Consultant,** Microscopy/Microscopy Education, Springfield, MA

Major in Ceramics Engineering

# Ceramics Engineer

## From Razor Blades to Microchips

Lisa Litz-Montanaro didn't think she wanted to be an engineer. She loved to "throw pots" (make pottery) in high school. She thought she might like to study fine arts in college. If not fine arts, maybe marine biology, which had fascinated Lisa since she was 10 years old. But Lisa has been working 17 years as a ceramics engineer and she loves it.

## Owes Her Fine Arts Teacher

Lisa says she owes her engineering career at least partially to a great fine arts teacher. In her senior year of high school, Lisa told her teacher, Mr. Goldberg, she was considering majoring in fine arts and teaching it, like he did. "The fine arts teachers are bussing tables," he said to her.

# LISA'S CAREER PATH

Throws pots and loves art    Gets ceramic engineering degree    Works as process engineer for fiber optics

"Okay," Lisa said. "If you're so smart, what should I study?" Her teacher saw Lisa's potential for engineering. He told her about a great engineering program at Alfred University in upstate New York, where he had gone to school. At the time Lisa was living in Westchester County, New York.

"You could study engineering, which will provide you with a good income. You'll have the flexibility to go into any industry you want, and you'll be set for life. You can take fine arts courses as electives and enjoy  your pottery in your spare time," Mr. Goldberg said. As it turned out, that's exactly what Lisa did.

Engineering wasn't exactly foreign to Lisa. Her father, a chemical engineer who has 35 patents in his name, and her mother, a musician and artist, didn't push her in any career direction. But they were pleased when she chose engineering.

"From the time my three sisters and I were teenagers, it was always made clear to us that we would all earn our own living and never have to depend on another person to support us. When we turned 16, all of us got jobs. Before 16, we ironed napkins for a penny apiece and tablecloths for a quarter. There was always an insistence on the value of doing work. Eventually, all my sisters ended up in technical or business fields."

Her oldest sister was already working in microscopy, the study of how to

use microscopes in industry and science. (Because of her sister's urging, Lisa attended a series of seminars at the Royal Microscopical Society in England the summer after her sophomore year of college.)

The first two years at Alfred University, Lisa studied all the time and took extra courses so that she would have the freedom to relax a little bit as an upper-class student. There were so many formulas to learn! In ceramic engineering, you study physics, inorganic chemistry, calculus, differential equations, and physical chemistry. "We memorized hundreds of reactions and understood the processing of many different types of materials."

## It All Made Sense

By her junior year, Lisa was having fun with her engineering courses. "I understood why we had to take those basics. My junior and senior electives were much more interesting and more pertinent. We had a ceramics fabrication class in which we learned all the different ways that ceramics are made, from extrusion and powder pressing to isostatic pressing. We studied fiber optics and semiconductor chips and the growing of crystals. We had labs where we actually extruded clay. In

a glass lab we made different types of glass and actually formulated the raw materials into a crucible. You put on this asbestos overall and took off all your jewelry and you basically just walked into a furnace. The guy behind you was there so that if your pants started smoldering, he could pull you out. With the hands-on work, you understood why you needed all the formulas. All at once the processes started making sense."

In her senior year, Lisa got a co-op position at General Electric. It lasted nine months and was great work experience and good money. Her work was to figure out why certain light bulbs that were packaged in large lots prior to assembly failed when it came time to assemble them but others in different lots did not. "I would recommend to anyone who has the opportu-nity to take a co-op to do so, because it tends to help crystallize your desire or lack of desire to continue in your field. I liked the detective part of it. For me, engineering has always been about problem solving."

## The First Job Interview

Since she was a college sophomore, Lisa had practiced job interviewing with recruiters who were seeking students to join their company. "There were a lot of jobs that sounded really boring. I didn't want to pursue them. I said to myself that I wanted to go into either fiber optics or computer chips— the two technologies that were the hottest, the most interesting, the most cutting edge."

At her initial interview with her first employer, a fiber optics manufacturing company, she sketched the manufacturing process as they described the way their fiber optics were made. "They explained to me that they made fiber optics with bunches of 10,000 fibers, each made of three layers of glass. The outside layer could be etched away to make the fibers flexible so you could gang together 10,000 of them. If you etched away the outer layer, they would flap against each other like hair. The second layer deflected light right back into the core. It was a reflective layer that would keep the intensity of the light from one end to the other the same. The third layer was the core glass that transmitted all this light. It was very clear glass. As they were talking, I was sketching what I thought would be the process. I showed them my sketch and I think they were very impressed. They said, 'well, we don't do it exactly like that, but you are very close.' I think my attitude and enthusiasm probably got me the job."

Lisa was the only process engineer working for the company. She had to analyze their manufacturing process

## CAREER CHECKLIST ✔

### You'll like this job if you ...

- Have patience

- Like working with tiny things like chips

- Are curious to know how things work

- Like using your hands

- Can analyze a problem with great insight

- Love science and high-tech gadgets

- Can think of better ways to do things

- Are fascinated with materials

# JOB FACTS

**HOURS:** 8:00 to 5:00

**WORKPLACE:** Home office
   Semiconductor plants and client's offices

**CLOTHES:** Business suit

**DUTIES:** Design procedures to analyze failure rates in manufactured products. Write training manuals and teach engineers failure testing.

**SALARY:** Ceramic engineer, average $31,500 to $55,000

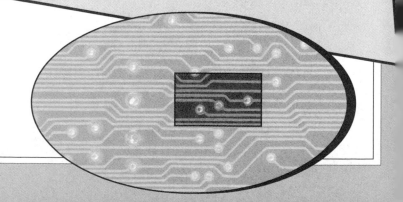

and recommend improvements. She ran into problems when she asked the people how much time it took to do things. They were afraid she was going to ask them to do their jobs faster. So she told them, "Build as much of a cushion into your estimates as you feel comfortable with. I just want to get an idea of how long it takes to manufacture a product, so that when we tell the Navy we can do

or judgment. It's not a productive approach."

As Lisa learned about how to improve manufacturing processes, she worked six days a week to get things done. After two years with the company, Lisa decided to look for better opportunities. Her first interview was with the Gillette Company. She got the job and moved to Boston.

> Two years ago the spacing between semiconductor features might have been .35 microns, about a third of a micron. Now the spacing is .17 microns, which means everything is closer and more tightly packed.

something in six weeks, it's not really eight weeks, or two weeks." That was Lisa's first experience in gaining cooperation by sharing her objectives with people and making them part of the process. "I don't ever resort to blame

## From Sharpened Sapphire to Failure Analysis

At Gillette, Lisa developed and processed ceramics for butane-powered curling irons, butane flashlights, and ceramic razor blades. "It was fun to develop products. One I worked on, the ceramic razor blade, might be coming on to the market soon. I can say, I did the work to develop that and evolved the process to where they could make that razor blade."

Lisa developed technology that would allow Gillette to sharpen sapphire, a hard material, to a point that would be good for shaving. Sapphire phire. Sapphire is so hard you need something very strong to grind it. You have to be careful, however, because you can damage it pretty easily in grinding."

After Lisa had been at Gillette five years, the company was at risk of a takeover, so it bought back much of its own stock to retain control. Management offered severance packages (extra money to leave the company) to

[ **You put on asbestos overalls and took off all your jewelry and you basically just walked into a furnace.** ]

razor blades last much longer than the razor blades now being sold to consumers because the sapphire is harder and doesn't get destroyed as easily. "I developed the sharpening tool. I worked to get the angle of the wheel to sharpen right, and then I worked with different manufacturers of the wheels to develop the right materials to perfect the sharpening and reduce the damage to the sap-

those who volunteered to leave, downsizing the company. Many people, including Lisa, took what was offered.

Next, Lisa took a job at the computer manufacturer IBM, where she learned to find the defects in ceramic packaging (the multilayered ceramic plate that is attached to the semiconductor chip). This "failure analysis" is a highly prized skill. It requires lots of problem solving and the ability to find out quickly why defects occur so that the manufacturing process can be improved.

Lisa's job at IBM was in Fish Kill, New York, where she bought her first

house using her severance pay. At a party one night, she met her future husband, Cosimo, who lived and worked in a town about two hours away. Cosimo is also an engineer. Lisa couldn't get Cosimo out of her mind. Finally, after nine months, she asked her friend for his telephone number. (She had never called a man for a date before.) She arranged to meet with Cosimo when she was in his area for business and to have dinner with him.

The dinner lasted until five o'clock in the morning! Lisa and Cosimo dated for about nine months, then they were engaged for a year, and then they married. But they were still living in separate houses in separate towns, because they both had jobs that they loved. They vowed that their next jobs would be where they could live together.

## Microchip Analysis in Virginia

A year later, when the couple had the opportunity to take jobs at the Dominion Semiconductor plant in Manassas, Virginia (a microchip factory that is owned by IBM and Toshiba), they jumped at the chance. Cosimo was hired for his chemical vapor deposition skills—taking gases and making them into thin layers that are then deposited on a silicon wafer. These layers are patterned and etched and built up into a microchip. Lisa was

hired for her failure-analysis skills. Lisa's job was to determine why the microchips, generally used in computers and to provide both logic and memory, failed. To do this, she had to carefully strip off layer by layer of the chip, pinpoint the actual cause of fail-

About every six months, the design of the chip would be changed. Chips are getting smaller and smaller, and the distance between the different areas on the chips is growing smaller too. The unlayering process that worked for one design of chips won't

> If we tried and couldn't find the problem, we would recommend they do this additional step and the problem would be completely gone. Even though adding that step is more costly, the fact that you have a solution is rewarding.

ure, and then work with the process engineers to correct the problem. Eighty percent of the time, the problem is a little bit of dust or other material that contaminates the chip. Lisa perfected a chemical process that would make the unlayering easier. But sometimes the particle that caused the failure wouldn't be there anymore, and she could only see the "footprint" of it. That made the work very challenging.

necessarily work for another. Failure analysis engineers are always inventing new unlayering techniques to test failures. That's part of what keeps the job interesting.

After two years, Lisa got a chance to do engineering consulting. She now works from an office in her home. She helps companies create and perfect ways to do failure analysis; she provides training on how to test; and she even does some market research for companies with new, emerging technologies. Lisa loves consulting, but she doesn't think she wants to do it for the rest of her life. "I find that I miss the corporate culture; the continual stimulation of working with other engineers," she says.

She and Cosimo haven't decided if they want to have kids. For now, they are just enjoying being together in their own house.

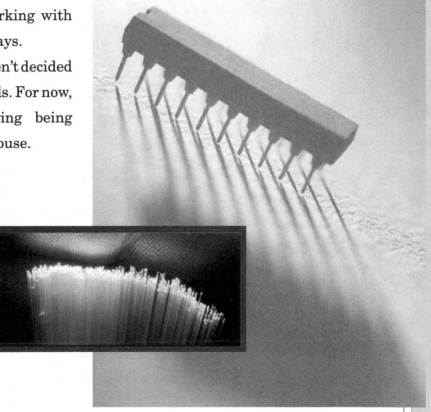

# Marti Hron

**Civil Engineer/Transportation Specialist,** Intelligent Transportation Systems, Federal Highway Administration, U.S. Department of Transportation Washington, DC

Major in Civil Engineering, master's degree in Civil Engineering

# Civil Engineer

## It's Not Your Grandfather's Highway Anymore

In the New York City area, over 5.5 million rides are taken each day on public transportation. That's one out of every three people using public transportation in the United States. Marti Hron is working with various transportation agencies in New York to provide information about how to go from point A to point B that can be shared with the people who use the New York/New Jersey/Connecticut public transportation systems. When this project is complete, New Yorkers, commuters, and visitors who come to the city will be able to find the shortest, most efficient way to get to their destination by checking a page on the Internet or calling a special telephone number.

The project is complex. It involves 28 different transportation agencies in New York, New Jersey, and Connecticut that coordinate the sharing of information with each other. Sometimes, the agencies will need to purchase new technology, such as computer software or automated voice-response systems. The agencies always have to dedicate some employees to providing and updating information like bus and train schedules, traffic accidents, burst water mains, heavy traffic, and other incidents that help to determine traffic and commuting patterns. Marti's job is to (1) make sure that everyone understands what needs to be done to share the information, (2) translate the concerns of various agency representatives to the rest of the group working on the pro-

ject, including representatives from state departments of transportation and metropolitan planning organizations, and (3) ensure that federal guidelines are met.

## What ITS is all About

Marti works on many projects in her job as a transportation specialist for the Federal Highway Administration. Marti works on the federal Intelligent Transportation Systems (ITS) program. ITS shows states and municipalities the "best practices" in managing public transit and highway traffic, by using technology and information. ITS employees help state departments of transportation and transportation agencies at the city and county levels learn about what

106

Starts taking
courses at college

Decides on Civil
Engineering, gets divorced

Graduate research
assistant, gets
master's degree

types of highway systems, public transportation systems, and technology will work best for them. For example, ITS employees might advise state employees about the best use of HOV signs (warning travelers of an accident or heavy traffic up ahead).

"It's not your grandfather's highway anymore," Marti says. "Our mission is to use advanced technologies to

> We are looking for civil engineers, computer specialists, electrical engineers, and people who have good communications and presentation skills.

(high occupancy vehicle) lanes, ramp metering (traffic lights that regulate the flow of traffic entering the highway), roadway surveillance cameras to detect accidents and other traffic "incidents," and variable message help states create and maintain efficient and safe highway and public transportation systems."

Marti is one of four ITS support people who work with federal employees in the states on transportation issues.

107

Joins FHWA,
▼ 18 months
Transportation Management
Training Program

Helps Atlanta
▼ prepare for Olympics, moves
to Washington, DC

She has responsibility for all of Virginia, West Virginia, New York, New Jersey, Massachusetts, Connecticut, Vermont, New Hampshire, Maryland, District of Columbia, Rhode Island, Delaware, Pennsylvania, and Maine. For the federal employees who work with state employees, Marti is a source of the ITS information they need to help the state create efficient transportation systems. Besides acting as a liaison and facilitator (like she does in New York) and providing information about current federal projects (like she does for federal field personnel), Marti helps field employees share with each other the information they learned while working with their respective transportation agencies.

## All in a Day's Work

On a typical day, Marti will take the bus from her apartment in Virginia to a subway station and then take the subway into Washington. She'll arrive at work about 7:30 a.m. She'll spend the first hour or so in her cubicle on her computer going through her email messages, learning about new ITS initiatives and answering questions from citizens who have written to the U.S. President or the Secretary of Transportation about transportation concerns. Sometimes she must get the right information to the United States Congress when members of Congress ask about a project she is involved in.

Today, Marti is recruiting students about to graduate from college for her organization. She finds resumes on the Internet by checking the various professional engineering societies and writes letters to students she thinks might be good candidates for the new employee program, an 18-month experience. "The training program is really good. Those selected will learn how ITS advanced technologies are used through 'hands on' experience with a state or local transportation agency. They will help develop and implement new ITS programs and policies in the Washington, DC, office as well as actually work with state and local agencies in the implementation of ITS projects with our field offices." To accomplish this, the training program is divided up into major segments, and the new employee will move to the different Federal Highway Administration offices within the United States. "We are looking for civil engineers, computer specialists, electrical engineers, and people who have good communications and presentation skills."

By mid-morning, Marti probably will go to a meeting, where she and her colleagues discuss the projects they are working on and talk about how to

# CAREER CHECKLIST ✓

## You'll like this job if you ...

- Can listen to people's concerns and express their worries accurately to others
- Are good at networking to get the information you need
- Can influence people
- Have a good grasp of physics and math
- Enjoy speaking to groups and moderating or facilitating discussions
- Will eagerly learn all the latest technology
- Are fascinated with how to move large numbers of people around efficiently
- Take the initiative to get things done!

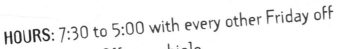

# JOB FACTS

**HOURS:** 7:30 to 5:00 with every other Friday off

**WORKPLACE:** Office cubicle
   Holds classes in field offices, works on train when
   traveling to New York

**CLOTHES:** Business clothes

**DUTIES:** Shares information about sophisticated technology
   called ITS (Intelligent Transportation Systems). Communicates
   federal guidelines to transportation professionals. Coordinates
   18-month Transportation Management Training Program.

**$ALARY:** $40,000 to $80,000

make things work more smoothly if there are problems. Then she may work on one of her special projects. For example, she recently participated in a train-the-trainer program designed to help field employees to better inform system. Marti has to know all these things and be able to explain them clearly to other people.

On days when she has a meeting in New York, Marti will drive to the train station in Washington at 7:00 a.m.

> While algebra and calculus had just been fun, like a foreign language but more of a game, when she got to the engineering courses and the physics, it all started to make sense.

transportation officials of the benefits of ITS. This training, which is designed to take an entire day, can be tailored by the federal employees in the field for their work with state Department of Transportation officials. Field employees may want to emphasize how the technology works today, or why it's important to share information with cities and other states, or how to build a good highway and take the train to New York. The meeting will take all day. She will return home that same day, arriving at the train station back in Washington at about 7:00 p.m. "Usually I read on the train—going to New York I review my notes, and coming back I review notes from the meeting or just relax."

Marti travels two or three times a month. If she is traveling for business and she has a free weekend, she sometimes will stay and see the sights in the location where her meeting is held (using her own money over the weekend) and then return Sunday night. That way, she gets to see different parts of the Northeast United States.

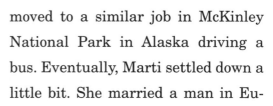

# The Travel Bug Got Her

Marti grew up in West Bend, Wisconsin. After high school, she had the urge to travel. She would work for a little while, and then take off to see some of the country. One summer, after hearing about a job from a co-worker in

West Bend who drove a bus in Yellowstone National Park, she applied for and got that very job. She had so much fun that after two summers she

moved to a similar job in McKinley National Park in Alaska driving a bus. Eventually, Marti settled down a little bit. She married a man in Eugene, Oregon, and got a job driving a city bus. She was one of the first women to drive a city bus in that town.

Marti had tried college earlier, but didn't like it. When she got older, she wanted to take some courses and try again. Her mother was a teacher and thinks education is very important, and Marti wanted to prove to both herself and her mother that she could pass college courses. She started with a pottery class, which she took for three semesters at the community college. Then she decided to try an algebra class.

physics course. While algebra and calculus had just been fun, "like a foreign language but more of a game," when she got to the engineering courses and the physics, it all started to make sense. "It became very real; there

> # You have to be able to say the right thing at the right time so that people will hear you. A lot of times that means saying it over and over again until they are ready to listen.

She liked it so well that she progressed to trigonometry and then took four semesters of calculus for the fun of it. She loved the math! Next she took chemistry, where she met a number of the students who were interested in engineering. She decided to try engineering too. She took an introductory series for engineers—courses in statics (which refers to stationary forces), dynamics, and strengths of materials engineering along with a

were applications for all the math that I had taken. That's when engineering became interesting."

## Why Civil Engineering?

Marti selected civil engineering as her major because she could concentrate on either structures (building bridges and other large outdoor structures) or transportation (she had hands-on experience as a bus driver), both of which fascinated her. By the time she had completed the first two years of requirements for the engineering degree at a community college, she decided to go back to school full-time. She was 38 years old, and she and her husband were divorcing. She finished her B.S. degree in civil engineering at Oregon State University and then became a graduate research assistant so she could get her master's degree. That took her one more year.

In her last semester at school, Marti sent out 20 resumes. She heard from three of the people she had mailed to, two consultants in Portland, Oregon, and the Federal Highway Administration, who all wanted to hire her. She chose the Federal Highway Administration program rather than the consultants because the federal government offered excellent training and travel. The government sent her to Baltimore for six months, then to Washington, DC, to the agency's headquarters, and then to Seattle for six months.

Marti's first assignment after she finished training was in Atlanta, Georgia, in 1994. She helped the city get ready for the traffic that would result when Atlanta hosted the 1996 Olympics. Marti was a project manager for the operational tests project Atlanta Driver, Advisory System which used Global Positioning System (GPS) software. This software, which is manufactured by private companies and now used in cars, allows a driver to map out a destination using a computer database. It features a map with an arrow that shows which way to travel. The driver also can hear a voice instructing her on where to turn to reach her destination. Marti's agency overlaid this commercial system with a system that reports traffic accidents and incidents, so that a driver would be able to avoid areas that were congested or blocked. Marti also was responsible for evaluating another project that was being tested in Atlanta by Georgia's Department of Transportation. She worked on the Atlanta Traveler Information Showcase Project where information about traffic was put on a

TV station, on the Internet, delivered to individual personal communication devices, and available through a hotel television channel. After 1996, Marti moved to Washington, DC, to her present job.

For fun, Marti still loves to travel with friends and steals away to West Virginia and Pennsylvania mountains with her friends as much as she can. Last year she got to go to France, and this past fall, she visited Puerto Rico for the first time.

# Carmella Apodaca

**Technical Support Specialist,** Natural Resources Conservation Service,
U. S. Department of Agriculture, Las Cruces, NM

Major in Civil Engineering

# Agricultural Engineer

## Waterwise

Carmella Apodaca figures out how to move water. She works in the state of New Mexico, a land of mountains and hills and desert, where the land can be rocky, clay, rich soil, or sand. She solves problems for the people who want to grow crops or raise animals. Most of those problems concern the use of the land and that vital necessity, water.

Carmella is the technical expert for eight field offices of the U.S. Department of Agriculture's Natural Resources Conservation Service (NRCS). Her office is in Las Cruces, and she works all over the southwestern part of New Mexico.

When people need help with a problem, such as getting water to their livestock out on the range, or they want advice on what type of irrigation

# CARMELLA'S CAREER PATH

Learns about
engineering in
summer program

Enjoys lots of
math in high
school

Graduates college

system they should put in, they contact the NRCS office. The people at the field office call for tech support, and that's Carmella. Sometimes she drives three or four hours to reach the

water to livestock, dams, and terracing for soil erosion control (so the water will move more slowly and won't take away so much soil). For most of the problems, Carmella starts

> You have to be tough and take some things from men you might not want to. It's not that they are sexist about women engineers, it's just that they may be overprotective, try to take care of you.

field office, then another hour or so out to the site to work on the problem.

Carmella has designed irrigation systems for farms, pipelines to get

out by evaluating and surveying the land to see the type of soil, the slope or how level it is, the way the water runs, what type of crop or livestock is

**Works in Arizona** on the
▼ floodways project

**Agricultural engineering** in
▼ Pacific area, learns scuba

**Various engineer**
▼ **jobs** California and
Arizona, part-time
travel agent

involved, and to get some ideas whether she can help the person do what they want done. Then, she makes recommendations for a number of alternatives with different costs.

For example, Carmella might be asked for help in bringing irrigation to a pecan orchard. She would have to know the type of soil (sandy, clay, or silt), so she could determine how fast the water would be absorbed into the soil. She would need to know how much water the pecan trees need to thrive, because different irrigation methods deliver water in different amounts. When Carmella has all the information, she makes some recommendations about what type of irrigation system to install. She might recommend a drip system as one al-

ternative and a sprinkler system as another alternative. She might even recommend flooding the field to irrigate it, depending on how level the land is and the location of the nearest water source. Carmella estimates what it will cost the farmer for her different recommendations. It is up to the farmer to decide how frequently he or she wants to irrigate and which type of method to install.

Carmella also designs pipelines. She's working on a pipeline that will take the water flowing within an irrigation ditch from one side of a river to the other so that the farmer can irrigate land on both sides of the river. Her pipeline will go under the river, deep enough so the land is stable and the river water won't wash the pipeline away. Getting the pipe under the river is a real challenge that requires calculating how to move the water from the river away from that area so the pipe can be installed. A pump will be used to divert the water while the pipeline is being placed.

## On the Road

Today, Carmella, who lives with her mother in Garfield, got up at 5:00 a.m. (her normal time). She left her house at 6:00 to drive the 50 miles to her office, arriving around 7:00 a.m. Then she grabbed the keys to the Tech Support car—a 4-wheel-drive Ford Bronco—and headed to a field office 80 miles away. She and two people from that office received and responded to a request from a farmer (another 40 miles away) who was losing crop land.

It was falling into a stream bed. Carmella and her colleagues looked at the stream and how the running water was eroding the bank. They took a survey of the land. They measured the slope of the stream bed and the depth where the water flowed. They evaluated where to put soil or rock to stop the water from eroding the land. Carmella sketched the problem on paper and began thinking about the recommendations she would make. She and the field representatives went back to the field office where she told them what she was going to recommend. Then she drove back to Las Cruces to her office and plotted the design on her computer using an auto-CAD (computer assisted drawing) system.

For every trip like this, Carmella must write a "trip report." She will write about the problem, her recommendations, and preliminary estimates of costs for each solution she proposes. Copies of the report will go to her boss and to the field representatives, who will share the information with the farmer. The farmer may decide to do nothing, but if the farmer chooses one of the recommendations, Carmella will go out to the farm again to do a more thorough survey. Then she will prepare final designs and costs. Later she will monitor the work, making sure it is being done correctly by the contractors the farmer hires to do it.

Every day it seems there are new and different projects and problems to solve. "The variety is the best part of my job," Carmella says. "I don't have to stay in the office all the time, or to be in the field all the time. When it's bad weather, I can stay in and work. When it's nice, I'll go to the field."

To do her work well, Carmella has to understand how water flows and the principles of physics. She has to know how to use the auto-CAD and other

## CAREER CHECKLIST ✓

# You'll like this job if you ...

Enjoy the outdoors

Are very good at math and understand physical concepts

Don't get easily offended and can take what people say with a grain of salt

Don't mind working with lots of men

Can communicate well with people

Want to understand the physical relationship of soil, water, and plants

Will learn computer software programs to do your job

# JOB FACTS

**HOURS:** Office hours 8:00 a.m. to 4:30 p.m.; usually works 7:00 a.m. to 6:30 p.m

**WORKPLACE:** Office with windows, lots of time spent driving and in the field

**CLOTHES:** Jeans and tennis shoes for the field and home office; business clothes (pantsuit or dress) for meetings with other government workers

**DUTIES:** Surveys land, recommends solutions to bring water to crops and animals, designs irrigation systems, meets with other federal, state, and city government representatives to discuss how irrigation systems may affect highway or other government-owned property. Writes reports of trips and recommendations.

**$ALARY:** $30,000 to $70,000

computer programs, and she has to know how to do the math calculations that will help her arrive at the right solutions.

# A Native New Mexican

Carmella grew up in Garfield and in Albuquerque, New Mexico. Her father was a farmer. She has three older

Carmella first got interested in engineering through a summer program called MITE (Minority Introduction to Engineering), which was an overview course of different types of engineering offered jointly by her high school and New Mexico State University at Las Cruces. Carmella learned a little about civil, mechanical, agricultural, industrial, chemical,

brothers. In high school, she was into everything—cheerleader, band, drill team, pep squad. She also played baseball, basketball, and volleyball.

She loved math, was the top math student in her class, and received a distinguished service award.

and electrical engineering. She liked civil engineering the best because it deals with structures. Another reason Carmella knew she would like civil engineering was because she could work outside part of the time. She wouldn't have to sit behind a desk all day. "That's okay for some people, but it's just not me."

Carmella attended college at New Mexico State University, and because NMSU is an agricultural school, she also got some exposure to agricultural engineering. In college she loved chemistry and computer classes. She took lots of math along with her engineering studies. "About all I can remember about college is studying very, very hard, and finding out that the math, which was harder, wasn't as enjoyable as in high school."

## A Change of Scene

Carmella's first job out of college was with the federal government in the Soil Conservation Service, which is now the NRCS. She had offers from the state government, too, but decided to go to work for the federal government because she liked to travel, and she knew the federal government would send her to other states. She started in Chandler, Arizona, just outside Phoenix, as an assistant project engineer. Her job was be aware of all the work being done to make sure that contractors were doing their jobs right. The project was the construction of a large floodway that would divert water from the towns of Phoenix, Apache Junction, and Chandler away from the cities and into the Gila River. Lots of concrete had to be placed to build the floodway.

After three years, Carmella was recommended for a job in Guam, an island in the Pacific Ocean. She also worked in the Northern Mariana Islands (Saipan, Tinian, and Rota), American Samoa, and Hawaii. Here her work was agricultural engineering, working with farmers to build sprinkler systems, waterways, and other irrigation systems. On her days off, she learned to scuba dive and went diving with friends (never alone). "I love meeting people and making new friends. I'm a people person, and I loved finding out about the culture there."

Each time Carmella wanted to move to a new job, she would check the list of positions that were open she wanted to be near her family.

In April 1998, Carmella attended her cousin's wedding and met John Irwin, now her husband. John is a software engineer with the government contractor Raytheon. Currently, he is working on an atoll in the Mar-

> # [ If you know your job and you do it right, eventually people come to respect you and your opinion. ]

through the federal government system and put in her application. She liked the variety of working in new locations and with new people.

After Guam came a job at another government agency, the Bureau of Indian Affairs, working on a big canal system that flows water through Central Arizona. Then Carmella applied for and got an agricultural engineering job in Northern California, back with her old agency, Natural Resources Conversation Service. After that, she applied for her current job near home, in Las Cruces, because shall Islands. Carmella takes vacation time to visit him. "He is the most wonderful and sweetest man in the world. I feel blessed to have the life that I have. I can live with my family, take care of my mother, do work I love, and be married to the greatest guy in the world. What more could you want?"

In her spare time, Carmella plans her future travels. (She used to work on weekends for a travel agency so she could get good rates.) When she isn't traveling or scuba diving, she likes to bicycle and hike.

# Getting Started On Your

# Own Career Path

# Getting Started On Your Own Career Path

## WHAT TO DO NOW

To help you prepare for a career in engineering, the women interviewed for this book recommend things you can do now while in school.

### Lisa Harmon, Mechanical Engineer, Entrepreneur

If you like to figure out how things work, set up a little work space for yourself. It can be as simple as a box you keep the stuff in and put under your bed to keep out of your mom's way. You could fix a lamp or experiment with light refraction. If you like to sew, then figure out how the sewing machine works.

If you like history, get a book and learn how things you are interested in were developed. Trial and error were instrumental in the development of great inventions.

### Tracey Smith, Electrical Engineer

Keep in mind you can be anything you want to be. You can accomplish anything you really want to accomplish. Don't let anyone ever discourage you from your dreams. Especially, don't let anyone tell you what you want to do "is not a girl thing."

### Heidi Bauer, Computer Engineer

Do something fun on the computer. Find the free tools on the Internet to build a Web page. Begin playing with these. You'll be surprised at what you can build.

### Marti Hron, Civil Engineer

This field is so wide and varied that you can go in many different directions with your education and still find a job. Find which technical courses you like by trying them. Study lots of math and science.

### Lisa Montanaro, Ceramics Engineer

Whatever you choose to study, don't get too bogged down in it. Remember it isn't the be all and end all of everything. Take some chances and some risks by exploring different areas. Employers like to know you are willing to take a risk.

**Joan Sanders, Biomedical Engineer, Researcher**

In high school it's hard. Lots of boys don't want to go out with girls who are good at mechanical things and sports. But you have to be true to yourself.

## MORE THINGS TO DO NOW

- Start a club with your friends who are interested in learning more about engineering.
- Read fiction (see our Recommended Reading) to get a sense of what engineers do.
- Participate in science fairs and regional and national competitions. You can use your ideas to build things.
- Ask your parents to discover if there are any summer "camps" that introduce engineering and math and science to middle school students. For example, in Maryland the Goddard Space Flight Center offers a 5-day Summer Institute for middle school girls who qualify.

## COURSES TO TAKE IN HIGH SCHOOL

Algebra I & II, trigonometry, biology, physics, social studies (3 units), fine arts/humanities (1-2 units), computer programming or applications, geometry, calculus, chemistry, English (4 units), foreign languages (2-3 units). (Recommended by the National Association of Professional Engineers.)

## RECOMMENDED READING

*The New Way Things Work* by David Macaulay. (1998). Boston: Houghton Mifflin Co.

*Turn on the Lights—From Bed* by Robert Carson. (1997). New York: Learning Triangle Press.

*Engineer from the Comanche Nation Nancy Wallace* by Mary Ellen Verheyden-Hilliard. (1985). Equity Institute Bethesda.

*Engineering Project for Young Scientists* by Peter Goodwin.

*Ms Engineer* by Harmon. Philadelphia, PA: Westminster Press.

**Murder Mysteries:**

*Engineered for Murder* by Aileen Schumacher. (1996). Write Way Press.

*Framework for Death* by Aileen Schumacher. (1998). Write Way Press.
    (Heroine is Tory Travers, a construction expert.)

*Emma Chizzit and the Mother Lode Marauder* by Mary Bowen Hall. Series. (1993).
Walker & Co. (Heroine is Emma who runs a crane house-wrecking service.)
*Current Danger* by Marilyn Wallace. (1998). Doubleday.
(Heroine is Claudia Miller, a building contractor.)
*Permit for Murder* by Valerie Wolzien. Series. (1997). Fawcett Books.
(Heroine is Josie Pigeon, head of an all-woman construction crew.)

**General References**
Web site on engineering especially for young adults: (www.discoverengineering.org)
*Encyclopedia of Career and Vocational Guidance.* (1997). Chicago: J. G. Ferguson.

*The Girl's Guide to Life How to Take Charge of the Issues that Affect You* by Chatherine Dee.
(1997). Boston: Little, Brown & Co.
Celebrates achievements of girls and women, extensive resources.

## NEED HELP WITH COLLEGE COSTS?

- Start searching for scholarship monies now. Many scholarships are exclusively for women. A good place to start is at your school or local library.
- Look at a reference book like *Peterson's Scholarships, Grants, and Prizes.* (1997). Princeton, NJ: Peterson's. Web site is (www.petersons.com)
- Use the Internet with the keywords "scholarships for women."

## PROFESSIONAL GROUPS

Many engineer groups have their own organization and Web site. Check these groups and others for career exploration information, local student chapters, scholarships, and study guidelines. For additional organizations, check your library for the *Encyclopedia of Associations*, published by Gale Research.

## GENERAL

**JETS, Inc. (Junior Engineering Technical Society)**
Offers broad range of brochures, books, and videos. Provides competitions and events for high school students.
1420 King St., Ste. 405, Alexandria, VA 22314-2794
(703) 548-5387, email jets@nae.edu
Web site: (www.asee.org/external/jets/)

### National Academy of Engineering

Has a special program: The Celebration of Women in Engineering. Check their Web site (www.nae.edu/cwe)

2101 Constitution Avenue NW, Washington, DC 20418

(202) 334-1605

### National Society of Black Engineers

Offers scholarships

1454 Duke St., P.O. Box 25588, Alexandria, VA 22313-5588

(703) 549-2207

### National Society of Professional Engineers

PE (professional engineer) certification program

1420 King St., Alexandria, VA 22314-2715

(703) 684-2800

### Society of Hispanic Professional Engineers

5400 Olympic Blvd., Ste. 210, Los Angeles, CA 90022

(213) 725-3970

### Society of Women Engineers

Offers certificate and scholarship programs

120 Wall St., 11th Floor, New York, NY 10005

(212) 509-9577

Web site: (www.swe.org)

## SPECIALTIES

### Alliance for Engineering in Medicine and Biology

1818 N Street, NW, Ste. 600, Washington, DC 20036

(202) 331-3500

### American Academy of Environmental Engineers

130 Holiday Ct., No. 100, Annapolis, MD 21401

(410) 266-3311

### American Ceramic Society

735 Ceramic Place, Westerville, OH 43081-8720

**American Institute of Aeronautics and Astronautics**
>   370 L'Enfant Promenade, SW, Washington, DC 20024-2518
>   (202) 646-7400

**American Institute of Chemical Engineers (see IEEE below)**
>   (212) 705-7338

**American Society of Agricultural Engineers**
>   2950 Niles Rd., St. Joseph, MI 49085-9659
>   (616) 429-0300

**American Society of Civil Engineers**
>   1015 15th St. NW, Ste. 600, Washington, DC 20005
>   (202) 789-2200

**American Society of Heating, Refrigeration and Air-Conditioning Engineers**
>   1791 Tullie Circle, NE, Atlanta, GA 30329-2305
>   (404) 636-8400

**American Society of Mechanical Engineers (see IEEE below)**
>   (800) The ASME, (212) 705-7722

**Biomedical Engineering Society**
>   P.O. Box 2399, Culver City, CA 90231
>   (310) 618-9322

**Institute of Electrical and Electronic Engineers (IEEE)**
Gives scholarships. There are many engineering groups at this same location.
>   345 East 47th St., New York, NY 10017
>   (212) 705-7338

**Institute of Transportation Engineers**
Has student chapters and a library.
>   525 School St., SW, Ste. 410, Washington, DC 20024
>   (202) 554-8050

**Society of Plastics Engineers**
>   P. O. Box 0403, Brookfield Center, CT 06804-0403
>   (203) 775-0471
>   www.ncnm.edu

# How COOL Are You?!

Cool girls like to DO things, not just sit around like couch potatoes. There are many things you can get involved in now to benefit your future. Some cool girls even know what careers they want (or think they want).

Not sure what you want to do? That's fine, too... the Cool Careers series can help you explore lots of careers with a number of great, easy to use tools! Learn where to go and to whom you should talk about different careers, as well as books to read and videos to see. Then, you're on the road to cool girl success!

Written especially for girls, this new series tells what it's like today for women in all types of jobs with special emphasis on nontraditional careers for women. The upbeat and informative pages provide answers to questions you want answered, such as:

- ✔ What jobs do women find meaningful?
- ✔ What do women succeed at today?
- ✔ How did they prepare for these jobs?
- ✔ How did they find their job?
- ✔ What are their lives like?
- ✔ How do I find out more about this type of work?

Each book profiles ten women who love their work. These women had dreams, but didn't always know what they wanted to be when they grew up. Zoologist Claudia Luke knew she wanted to work outdoors and that she was interested in animals, but she didn't even know what a zoologist was, much less what they did and how you got to be one. Elizabeth Gruben was going to be a lawyer until she discovered the world of Silicon Valley computers and started her own multimedia company. Mary Beth Quin grew up in Stowe, Vermont, where she skied competitively and taught skiing. Now she runs a ski school at a Virginia ski resort. These three women's stories appear with others in a new series of career books for young readers.

The Cool Careers for Girls series encourages career exploration and broadens girls' career horizons. It shows girls what it takes to succeed, by providing easy-to-read information about careers that young girls may not have considered because they didn't know about them. They learn from women who are in today's workplace—women who know what it takes today to get the job.

## EACH BOOK ALSO INCLUDES:

✔ A personality checklist for each job

✔ Lists of books to read and videos to see

✔ Salary information

✔ Supportive organizations to contact for scholarships, mentoring, or apprenticeship and intern programs

## THE BOOKS ALSO LOOK AT:

✔ What skills are needed to succeed in each career
✔ The physical demands of the different jobs
✔ What the women earn
✔ How to judge whether you have the personality traits to succeed in the different jobs
✔ How much leisure time you'll have
✔ How women balance work and relationships
✔ Reasons for changing jobs
✔ The support received by women to pursue their goals
✔ How women handle pregnancy and child care
✔ What you need to study to get these jobs and others

## So GET WITH IT!
### Start your Cool Careers for Girls library today...

## ORDER FORM

| Title | Paper | Cloth | Quantity |
|---|---|---|---|
| Cool Careers for Girls in Computers | $12.95 | $19.95 | _____ |
| Cool Careers for Girls in Sports | $12.95 | $19.95 | _____ |
| Cool Careers for Girls with Animals | $12.95 | $19.95 | _____ |
| Cool Careers for Girls in Health (June 1999) | $12.95 | $19.95 | _____ |
| Cool Careers for Girls in Engineering (July 1999) | $12.95 | $19.95 | _____ |
| Cool Careers for Girls with Food (August 1999) | $12.95 | $19.95 | _____ |
| | **SUBTOTAL** | | _____ |

VA Residents add 4½ % sales tax
Shipping/handling $5.00+                                                    $5.00
$1.50 for each additional book order ( __ x $1.50 )

**TOTAL ENCLOSED**                     _____

SHIP TO: (street address only for UPS or RPS delivery)
Name: _____
Address: _____

❏ I enclose check/money order for $ ____made payable to Impact Publications
❏ Charge $ ____to: ❏ Visa ❏ MasterCard ❏ AmEx ❏ Discover

Card #: _____ Expiration: _____
Signature: _____ Phone number: _____

one toll-free at 1-800/361-1055, or fax/mail/email your order to:
.pact Publications
04-N Manassas Drive, Manassas Park, VA 20111-5211
x: 703/335-9486; email: orders@impactpublications.com